C000091304

RIVALS

Football Fans Love-Hate Games

MARTIN KING

Head-Hunter Books

First published in November 2004, this paperback edition 2006.
by Head-Hunter Books
PO Box 26066
London SW10 0XP

Copyright © 2004 Martin King

The moral right of the author has been asserted

All rights reserved. No part of this publication may be reproduced in
any form or by any means without permission in writing from the
publisher, nor be otherwise circulated in any form of binding or
cover other than that in which it is published and without a similar
condition being imposed on the subsequent purchaser.

ISBN 0-9548542-6-8

Head-Hunter Books

All the illustrations in this book are by Martin King.
Every effort has been made to contact the relevant copyright holders
of the illustrations used on the jacket, the publisher would be grateful
for any information.
Author photograph by Julia Rowley

Printed in Great Britain by Creative Print and Design Ltd

Acknowledgements

I would like to thank Pete Walsh from Milo Books for all his help and advice, me old mate, Fat Pat Dolan, Gill from Wolves, Boatsy from Forest, Monty and Skeeny from Newcastle, and Nick and the Barnsley crew for helping me track down people for this project. Without that lots help and encouragement the book wouldn't have happened. Thanks for the support of Dave at the CFCUK fanzine and the love and help of Mandy, Kortney and the next middle weight champion of the world, Rory-Ben King. A big thank you too Kate for all your help and hard work, you're a star, and to everyone who buys the books and likes them, and to Sarah Jessica Parker. What happened to my mention? And to all the passers by and to my dogs, Barney, and Posh.............zzzzzzzzzz

Contents

This book is dedicated to John Bloomfield, a good friend, who sadly passed away on the 17th September, 2004. My family and me have lots of happy, fond and funny memories of John. He was a well-respected and successful boxing trainer who had worked with some of the best amateur and professional boxers from all over the country. Frank Bruno, Andy Till, Rocky Kelly, Michael Sprott, to name just a few. He had a terrific sense of humour and was well liked by everyone, as the turn out for his funeral showed. God bless ya mate, you'll be forever in our thoughts. We never did do that book together but not to worry, gel on cuz.

R.I.P.

THE FANS

Cass Pennant

Ginger Bob

Chelsea Dave

Gaz Rayner

Wilmot

Tommo

Dan Moore

Michael Aronoffsky

Bonzo

THE FANS

Randolph Campbell

Abbo

The Belly

Choco

Palmer

Barry (Larry)
Lawrence

Gregor

Pot

Johnie

Jimmy The Jock

Ricky

Rob Silvester

Ray

Sesh

Ducker

Matt

Brighton Ben

Introduction

Introduction

Watching live football these days 'as never been safer, or so we are led to believe. More women and children are attending games, arrests are down and high profile policing and CCTV cameras have gone a long way in the fight against stamping out hooliganism. Along with all seated and all ticket stadiums and stricter segregation, the game 'as attracted a whole new audience. The bad old days we are told, are over. No more hordes of fighting youths on concrete terraces, no more pitched battles behind the goal posts as brave policemen, unconcerned for their own safety, dive into the swaying, boisterous crowds followed closely in attendance by St. John ambulance men ready to swathe someone's cracked skull in bandages. No more bewildered players, hands on hips, looking on as offenders are arrested and dragged from the melee with arms up their backs whilst being frog marched backwards around the edge of the pitch and out of the ground, never to be seen again. Their one-minute of fame is over and a ten-year banning order awaits them at a court appearance in front of a furious Beak. Nevertheless, in some matches, even in the current climate of the prawn sandwich, corporate entertainment game, you will still get feelings running high. Despite what we are told, football, like it or not, is still a highly charged spectator sport where singing, swearing, shouting and chanting are the norm, or they are when you play your local rivals. They are the team you just love to beat, a game more important to some than life or death. Rivalry exists in all aspects of life, in schools, in the work place, the office, in pubs, it's every-where; be it playing netball, cards, snooker, or bingo, but it's with football where it goes up another gear and the hatred begins to creep in. Football rivalry may be geographical with your fiercest rivals maybe coming from just up the road, or they may be your hated rivals because you have a history against them. They may have dumped you out of a Cup competition or even worse, beaten you in a semi or God forbid, a final. They may have sent you down in a relegation battle or even some-thing simple like your neighbour supports them and you can't stand him, or because the opposition are always winning tro-phies and titles and their fans don't stop gloating about it. For some teams and some fans the rivalry runs even deeper. It may be religion, it may stem from a picket line being crossed or some sort of industrial action, or one town or city helping the Round Heads and the other supporting the Vikings. I kid you not, these things go deeper than you could ever believe which, over the years, has created not just a dislike for one another but in some cases, pure hatred. People have sadly lost their lives because they've supported a different football team from someone else. In July the new seasons' fixtures are published and this is the time when people are pencilling the dates of the big games against their rivals, into their diaries and onto calendars. These are the games they can't wait for, the games they love to hate.

Told by real fans and in their own words, not by some professor from a Midlands university who's developed a guessing strate-gy on what goes on amongst football fans and is like a leech who makes a living out of talking total bollocks, we find out why the hostilities still go on between clubs. We find out whether rivalry is the same thing as hooliganism. Are the hooligans being driv-en underground? The fans in these pages tell of new police tac-tics and new government laws, but are they winning the battle?

Just recently a firm of about seventy Chelsea took on a huge, thousand-strong, Paris Saint Germain mob in the streets of Paris and by all accounts done well until they pushed their luck just that bit too far. Millwall also took a thousand-strong mob out to Hungary for their European game. Would numbers like that still turn out in this country or would they even be allowed to? Are the old days far behind us?

In these pages I've interviewed a cross section of people. Some of them are just ardent fans that love their club and are what people would call normal supporters, and some are hooligans and top boys at their clubs who, by their own confessions, aint that keen on football and just go for the violence. They come from all walks of life and age groups and some are unemployed. The rest do a whole host of jobs but the one thing they have in common is that they all hate their rivals. Now, before certain so-called experts, and the "anoraks", and the "keyboard warriors" come out with the same old chestnuts "he aint a top boy" or "how come so and so aint in it?", and "he's no-one, he's just a mug", I asked many people for their views and some wanted to do it and others were not interested, it was as simple as that. One belief that came out perfectly clearly, even by the people who went just to watch the football and not get involved in the tear-ups, was that rivalry will always exist in the game of football as it does in all areas of everyday life.

Dictionary definitions

RIVAL - A person or group that competes with another for the same object or in the same field. To try to equal or surpass.

RIVALRY - Active competition between people or groups.

FOOTBALL - Any of various games played with a ball in which two teams compete to kick, head or propel the ball into each other's goal.

FAN - A person who admires or is enthusiastic about a pop star, actor, sport, or hobby.

HATE - To dislike someone or something.

PART ONE

WEST HAM

RI  ALS

MILLWALL

Name: **Cass Pennant**

Club: **West Ham United**

We Mobbed Up At! I've known Cass a few years now and we done a bit together in F.H.M. magazine. We also done a Writers' Festival up in Liverpool where between us we came up with the idea for the book "Terrace Legends". Because of all the politics involved some people doubted the project would get off the ground. Well, we proved them wrong with a best seller. I met up with Cass over at his house in South East London where he is putting the finishing touches to not one, but two books, the legendary Bill Gardner's story and the follow up to "Terrace Legends", which is "Top Boys".

History/Honours? 1964 '65, '66 we done the treble, the F.A. Cup, the Cup Winners' Cup and the World Cup. That's the West Ham treble and we done it well before Man. United, and a couple of F.A. Cups since. The Club started off as the Thames Iron Works team from Canning Town in 1985 but became West Ham United in 1900.

Background?   I was born in Doncaster and moved to East London when I was six weeks old, 46 years ago. I went to school in Slade Green, Erith, Kent. I've spent half me life in South East London and Kent, and half over in East London. I'm now a full time author after the big success of "Cass", "Congratulations", "Want Some Aggro?" and the "657" and "Terrace Legends" books.

Biggest rivals?   Millwall

First game you ever went to?   I went with a neighbour of mine when I was eight years old and he took me over to West Ham, although at the time my favourite player was Jimmy Greaves. I used to be glued to the TV when he appeared on the football programme, "The Big Match". I also liked Wolves because of the kit they wore. I used to like going over West Ham because it meant I got half a crown more pocket money a week to go to football with. At the time Harry Rednapp and John Sissons were just coming into the team and back then it was the wooden rattles, horse manure, and the smell of hot dogs. It was a different world.

Memories of first game against rivals?   Harry Cripps's Testimonial in '72. I went by bus with me mates from Woolwich when I was fourteen years old. As soon as we got to News Cross we were recognised and it kicked off. People were getting in through the emergency exits and it was going right off. We got split up and I decided to make my way to the ground. Everybody was eying up one another with suspicion and I tried to pick out faces I might know but blank faces stared back at me. As I got near to the ground you could sense the evil in the air and word was everyone was meeting in the Cold Blow Lane.

There were no colours, no singing, just strange faces. I met up with a few West Ham boys and we were pushed into the away end. I thought it would be packed with our boys but just like outside, no one was letting on who was who. An eerie "Millwall, Millwall" chant drifted across the terraces, our end remained silent, and people around started asking the lot I was with who we were. Being big, being black and being young, I stood out and for the umpteenth time I was asked who I was with. We were getting dug out and it seemed all of London had turned out for this one. Geezers from Tottenham, Arsenal and Charlton told us they were with us but when the fighting started you saw them swop sides and it was going off all over the place. Some serious, older Wes Ham faces began to dig me out not believing I was West Ham. I decided to leave the ground as I had half of London on me case and me own fans were accusing me of being Millwall and Millwall wanting to batter me. I'd had enough I'm not ashamed to say. Outside there were little skirmishes going on here and there and I bumped into a few of me mates from the bus with a few of the older lot from Woolwich. We walked around the ground and into the C.B.L. The game had kicked off and we made our way up the stairs until a wall of bodies stopped us going any further. We could hear the West Ham fans inside the mass of bodies which were going side to side and backwards and forwards, but we managed to get in and pushed and punched our way to where our boys were stood. It looked like the C.B.L. was split fifty fifty and it was to-ing and fro-ing with West Ham gaining ground and then Millwall regaining it with another surge. Outside it was more chaos with horses charging along the dark roads. It turned into a bit of a free for all with some West Ham hitting other West Ham, tools were being used and people were getting seriously hurt. West Ham claimed the result and took the C.B.L. but Millwall regained it and forced West Ham into the corner. Around about half time the Mile End boys came in tooled up where they've broke into a tool shed at White Chapel Station. They piled in straight down the middle with spanners, shovels and pickaxes and attacked everyone within range. They were a unique firm who were the governors at West Ham. No one fucked with the Mile End boys. Even the rest of the West Ham boys knew who ran the show. It was the battle to see who was the top firm in London and the Mile End came out winners. The game was such a bloodbath and it was the start of the modern day bad feeling between the Clubs.

Finest team performance against them? I can't remember a single team performance against Millwall; the score don't matter. This game is like no other game; it's the only game I know where the players are sometimes intimidated. This game is not for the normal supporters; people are there for one thing only.

Best goal? The football match itself is not talked about.

Worst defeat? Last season's 4-1 defeat.

Biggest crowd? We've got the bigger ground but lots of normal fans don't turn up for the Millwall fixture for the simple reason that this game is for the serious people only. You take the attendances for other London Derbies and they're up on the Millwall fixture for the simple fact that it's the serious faces day out when we play them. Look when they played us at the New Den. There was only thirteen thousand there but a few weeks later they wanted thirty thousand tickets for the Cup Final.

Best row, inside or outside the ground? Well there's obviously the Harry Cripps Testimonial and the Bobby O'Neil Testimonial, which a lot of fans thought was for their Barry Kitchener, and there's also the 1978 game at Upton Park which was the biggest police operation at the time for a football match. It was the first time a helicopter had been used to monitor the trouble, plus it was rumoured that there was one policeman for each Millwall fan. A small pocket of West Ham fans came up from the front of the South Bank and steamed into Millwall. The Old Bill put a thin blue line down the middle to try to split the warring factions but the battle went on throughout the game. Also there's been tit for tat fights after the death of a Millwall fan.

Have you ever been injured at a game, or nicked?   I've been bricked on the head at Chelsea, stabbed at Bristol City, slashed at Liverpool, and been nicked a few times, mostly on very serious charges.

What are your Old Bill like? They're on top and clued up but are fair. We used to think at one time that they favoured the away team. Not a lot goes on at home now anyway.

Name a player from their team you dislike or hate I admire a few of their players and I see things in some of their players that I see in West Ham's players. For a start a few of them are like fans who are turning out for the team they look like dockers and builders. I was a big fan of Keith Weller and Barry Kitchener as they were fans first and players second and they actually played for their fans.

Your favourite all time player?   Trevor Brooking, he had a talent, a gift mixed with leadership qualities. He could put the ball on a sixpence and to me he walked on water; he had that something a bit different.

Have any of their managers, past or present, really got up your nose? Never been interested in any of their managers. They were faceless. I never noticed the likes of George Graham or Frank McLintock when they were there. They are a London team going nowhere.

The worst song or chant their fans sing?   The one that winds some people up is the "Bobby Moore" song but it don't bother me, but they should remember he captained the England team to the 1966 World Cup, something no other England captain 'as ever done.

Your favourite song or chant about them? It's bang out of order, but some of our boys sing about the death of one of theirs at New Cross, and also "Chim Chimney Chim Chimney Charoo, We are Those Bastards in Claret and Blue," is another favourite when we play them.

What's the furthest you've travelled to watch your team? Carlisle in my younger days. It was like something off a cartoon train with sheep and smog and endless fields, and I've also watched the Hammers in Belgium, Holland and Germany, in our European campaigns.

Are you a season ticket holder, and do you think your Club could do more for its fans? Yea, I've got a season ticket and to me most football clubs should remember that the fans are the club.

Have you ever worn a replica shirt? No, never worn a shirt to a game but I've worn the England shirt to the pub when there's been a game on, and I do like the old fashioned West Ham replica shirt, I think that looks good. I also like the West Ham Club badge done as a tattoo. I haven't got it but I have got one with two arms linked with the words "Peace, Love and Understanding" on it. It cost me £17.

Have you ever cried at a game? No, never, but when we've lost big games I feel gutted. When we lost to Liverpool in the League Cup final replay I felt like my heart had been ripped out and I was like a bear with a sore head for days afterwards.

Do you take your children to football? I take my son who's now sixteen. He's been going since he was seven. Some of his mates from school only watch the games on Sky and support all the glory hunting Clubs, but my boy's stayed loyal to Westham even though we haven't done an awful lot these past few years.

What would you do if a family member married a Rival?   If my daughter married a Millwall fan I can say I wouldn't be happy but I wouldn't take offence. There's a lot more important things to worry about in life than the team someone supports. Anyway, you don't listen to women when it comes to football. What do they know about the game?

Do you look out for any other teams' results?   I've always had a soft spot for Charlton and look out for how they're doing, and Portsmouth because of the Harry Rednapp link.

Are there any other teams you dislike?   Yea, any team besides West Ham that are successful and get too big for their boots. I like the underdog and I hated the Liverpool, Man. United dominance.

If there's one player in the world, past or present, that you could sign, who would it be?   George Best or Pele. They were the world's greatest. They could beat people with ease and it was a joy to watch them dribble the ball past people, not like today where it's all about pace and muscle. The skilful ball players are now rare.

If you had the choice of the National team winning the World Cup or your side winning the Premiership, which would you choose?   West Ham, it's got to be club before country I'm afraid.

Would you ground share with your rivals?   Never, it would be the end of football as we know it. It would be like the protestant church and the catholic churches merging together. You can't mess with tradition and football is all about its' local community and where its' fan base comes from. It's above making money. Look at Charlton, when they ground shared they lost nearly all their fans. When they went back to their spiritual home, The Valley, the fans poured back in their droves. That's why almost all old stadiums are built in the very heart of the community. It used to be work Monday to Friday, football Saturday and church on Sunday. No, clubs must keep their own identities and not share stadiums.

Name: **Ginger Bob**

Club: **Millwall**

We Mobbed Up At! We met in a pub in Sheperds Bush. I'd been introduced to Bob by Fat Pat and here's what he said about his mad, mad Millwall days.

History/Honours? None to speak of, only an F.A. Cup Final appearance against Man. United 2003 – 2004 season. Qualified as losing finalists for the UEFA Cup competition for the first time in the Club's 117-year history.

Background? I was born in 1958 and lived in Peckham. I have a younger brother. I went to school in Lambeth and left with 5 'O' levels in Maths, English, Biology, Geography and Religious Education. Job wise I've done loads; I've been in printing, an apprentice electrician, the Post Office for 17 years and left in '91. Since then I've been doing bouncing, door work, minding, a bodyguard, and even a bit of mini-cabbing. I've done wrestling and weights just to keep fit and up for the job.

Biggest rivals?   West Ham. I hate them with a passion.

First game you ever went to?   Would have been around 1964 and it was Oxford United at home. I went with my dad when I was about six years old. In the team were people like Reg Davies the goalkeeper, Tommy Wilson, Brian Snowdon, the legendary Harry Cripps, Glen Juliens, and from then on I was hooked.

Memories of first game against rivals?   My first memories of West Ham were not when we played them but the fights with them before we'd ever played them in a match. The mid seventies was when we first played them due to the fact that they were in the old First Division and we were in the old Second Division, but we had many a battle with them at Surrey Docks and Rotherhithe and Wapping on the way back from games. We had a big off with them in '71. They were all tooled up and done well to start with, that was until we got our act together and ran them everywhere.

Finest team performance against them?   The 4-1 win last season at our place. It could have been worse for them because we missed two penalties.

Best goal?   Christian Dailley's own goal at the above game. (Hoots of piss take laughter!).

Worst defeat?   We lost 3-0 over there in about '78-'79.

Biggest crowd?   At Upton Park about 36,000, at the Old Den it would be about 24,000. Well that was the official figures, but thousands more got in after a gate was kicked in and fans steamed in without paying.

Best row, inside or outside the ground? About six top rows come to mind, all equally as good. A good one was '84. They were playing Crystal Palace and all their top boys, a full firm, Cas, Gardner, Teddy Bunter, The Birdman, about 350 of them, got off at New Cross Station and walked down towards New Cross Gate where about 60 of us were plotting up in a pub. A lot of our main faces hadn't arrived yet but we were well tooled up and nearly every one of us had either a baseball bat or a hammer or some sort of tool. We steamed straight into them and as their front row stood frozen, the ones at the back were concertinaed into one another. They had nowhere to run and took a right hammering and had the shit kicked out of them. One of their black boys got done with a milk crate and was in hospital for a fair while in a terrible state. They did try to come back at us but our main boys had turned up and they took another beating. The following week they waited for us at London Bridge. We were playing Sheffield United, there was fifty of us and about 150 of them and it was their turn to get tooled up. I'd missed the first train, the boys had gone on, but when I got there it was like a scene from Northern Ireland. The streets looked like Belfast with bricks and broken glass scattered all over the place and our boys had been run everywhere. I got everyone together and we charged back at them and run them in all directions. The only thing stopping us going right through them was one of them threw a petrol bomb which stopped us in our tracks. The row was a bit different to how they described it in their book "Congratulations You've Just Met the I.L.F.", pure fiction, total bollocks, a fucking load of shit.

Have you ever been injured at a game, or nicked? I've never been injured, but I did have two of their well-known faces trying to stick me with blades at the Testimonial in '75. I was only 17 at the time. We'd surrounded them in the Cold Blow Lane end of the ground and I'd faced up to Gardner who'd spat on the ground in front of me when I told him I was Millwall. The Old

Bill dragged me out and threw me out of the ground. In them days you just paid at the turnstile and came back in again. In the second half of the game I've got back in the middle of them and they've spotted me and came straight at me. Me and Stevie Merritt, a big, Millwall, Cockney Jewish boy who weighed in at nearly 30 stone and sadly died in '93 from cancer, steamed up the terraces at them and it went toe to toe with us slowly backing them up before the Old Bill broke it up.

What are your local Old Bill like?   They're against us all the time, they're the same as the media and our Chairman, they hate us.

Name a player from their team you dislike or hate   Teddy Sherringham.

Your favourite all time player?   Barry Kitchener, he loves the Club. I was in the stands up at Old Trafford with him when we got through to the Cup Final. He played for Millwall all his playing career, and even when a big money move was on for him to go to Liverpool, he chose to stay at Millwall. He loves the Club and the fans, and we love him. He's like family.

Have any of their managers, past or present, really got up your nose?   Yeah, Billy Bonds. Happy Harry Rednapp and his happy hammers and Alan Pardew. What I think of them is unprintable'

The worst song or chant their fans sing?   They just sing and chant scum at us and we call it back to them. We also call them vermin.

Your favourite song or chant about them?   The Bobby Moore song's great, it goes "Bobby Moore, Bobby Moore, running from the Den, Bobby Moore, Bobby Moore he had sex with men,

Queer as they come, Takes it up the bum, Bobby Moore, Bobby Moore, Bobby Moore". The cunts hate that one.

What's the furthest you've travelled to watch your team? Probably Carlisle with Millwall but with England, further.

Are you a season ticket holder, and do you think your Club could do more for its fans? Never had the money to buy a season ticket. We have the most loyal, working class fans in the country. No one likes us and the entire publicity correct brigade calls us racist. We love our team and if we had a Chairman to match our loyalty and support we'd go much further, someone like the Palace Chairman, who don't mind putting his hand in his pocket instead of take, take take. The Club's not in debt but we don't spend a penny on quality players. Now that Tim Cahill's gone where will that money go? Not on fucking new players that's for sure. We made five million from the F.A. Cup run. Where's that gone? To pay debts we're told. Debts my arse. The Club's being ruined by one man.

Have you ever worn a replica shirt?   No never. When scarves and colours were worn in the 70s I used to wear a satin scarf.

Have you ever cried at a game?   Yeah, I cried at the semi-final win last season. I've been told that only real men cry.

Do you take your children to football?   I have done. I took my little girl when we played Palace and she loved it, the songs, the hot dogs, yeah she loved it.

What would you do if a family member married a Rival? The past is the past. Certain political events which are happening in this country are far more important than football.

Do you look out for any other teams' results?   Yeah, to see if West Ham has got beat.

Are there any other teams you dislike?   Newcastle and Birmingham.

If there's one player in the world, past or present, you could sign who would it be?   Maradona in his prime when he was about 24-25.

If you had the choice of the National team winning the World Cup or your side winning the Premiership, which would you choose?   Millwall to win the Premiership. I'm very patriotic but I would love Millwall to win something. I love England and I love being English, but Millwall's me Club.

Would you ground share with your rivals?   I would but how long would it be before it was torn apart?

PART TWO

CHELSEA

RI VALS

TOTTENHAM

Name: **Chelsea Dave**

Club: **Chelsea**

We Mobbed Up At! At the C.F.C. U.K. stall on the Fulham Road. Chelsea are playing hosts to rivals Spurs and through the noise of police sirens and policeman rushing through the packed streets to save the Spurs fans, Dave tells me about his beloved Chelsea.

History/Honours? 1955 League Championship, 1965 League Cup, 1970 F.A. Cup, 1971 Cup-winners' Cup, 1997 F.A. Cup, 1998 League Cup, 1998 Cup-Winners' Cup, 2000 F.A. Cup plus Full Members' Cup winners. Losing F.A. finalists on many occasions and runners up in the Premiership 2003-2004.

Background? Born in Queen Charlotte's Hospital in West London where royalty are born. I'm 40 years old and became a top ragger when I was aged between 14 and 18. I never missed

a Chelsea game home or away, all financed by my skill as a
shoplifter. When I left school I worked as a porter in a hotel and
I'm now a successful businessman, but don't tell the Social!

Biggest rivals?   Tottenham Hotspur.

First game you ever went to?   Against Spurs in 1968 and it was
a 2-2 draw.

Memories of first game against rivals?   We used to live in
Victoria and we only had a very small back garden where me
and me dad used to kick a ball about along the path. Me dad
didn't like football so me Nan's neighbour took me and another
kid. We stood at the bottom of the Shed and when something
happened the kid with me shouted out "you bastard" and the
geezer that took us cuffed him around the head for swearing.

Finest team performance against them?   Either the 4-0 win or
the 6-1 win at Three Point Lane. My mate from Rayners Lane
was in with all the Spurs fans and led the chorus ob boos as the
Spurs side left the pitch at the final whistle. They pissed themselves laughing as everyone around them joined in the booing.

Best goal?   Eidur Gudjohnsen's goal at Three Point Lane in the
F.A. Cup.

Worst defeat?   Fuck me that's the League Cup semi-final.

Biggest crowd?   Sixty odd thousand in the 70s.

Best row, inside or outside the ground?   1978-1979. We lost 3-1
and it all kicked off in the North Stand and our lot were battling
with the police in the West Stand to get at them. It was going off
mental and outside there were running battles.

Have you ever been injured at a game, or nicked? 1977. It was Tuesday night in the League Cup up at Anfield and we'd lost 2-0. I was walking along the Scotland Road and I got hit with a brick on the head. There was a lot of blood and it sparked me for a minute but I got up and was as right as rain, but I had to have seven stitches in the wound.

What are your local Old Bill like? Fair to some people and not so fair to others.

Name a player from their team you dislike or hate. All of them.

Your favourite all time player? John Terry. He 'as my tee shirts and fanzines off me, he's a top bloke.

Have any of their managers, past or present, really got up your nose? I once rang up Richard Littlejohn on the radio. They were going on about Christian Gross and I phoned in and said what a great job he was doing at Spurs. "Are you an Arsenal fan?" asked Richard. "No, Chelsea" I replied and they used that conversation as a trailer on the show for weeks afterwards.

The worst song or chant their fans sing? I've never heard them sing.

Your favourite song or chant about them? "You'll Never Beat the Chelsea".

What's the furthest you've travelled to watch your team? Russia.

Are you a season ticket holder, and do you think your Club could do more for its fans? Yes I am a season ticket holder and the club could perhaps lower admission prices and charge less for the kids and treat fans with a bit of respect.

Have you ever worn a replica shirt? No never, fuck that.

Have you ever cried at a game? Maybe when I was a kid.

Do you take your children to football? No aint got any but if there's a woman out there who wants to go halves on one then give us a ring. I'm a bit of a stud between the sheets so get dialling girls!

What would you do if a family member married a Rival? It wouldn't happen.

Do you look out for any other teams' results? Millwall. I know the granddad over there who's a mate of mine, and Glasgow Rangers which always remind me of my mate, big Alan Ogilvie.

Are there any other teams you dislike? Man. United and Middlesborough.

If there's one player in the world, past or present, that you could sign, who would it be? I'd re-sign Zola, the perfect player on the pitch and a gentleman off of it.

If you had the choice of the National team winning the World Cup or your side winning the Premiership, which would you choose? Chelsea for the title.

Would you ground share with your rivals? No, you're fucking joking.

Name: **Gaz Rayner**

Club: **Tottenham Hotspur**

We Mobbed Up At! We met up for a drink in a social club on the South Coast. The night we met there was a pool match going on and a few of the home team had Spurs shirts on. A Yid stronghold on the South Coast? Read on!

History/Honours? The old Championship twice, the first team to do the double, the only team to win the F.A. Cup as a non-league side, a cup we've won 7 times, the League Cup a couple of times, and the U.E.F.A. Cup a few times.

Background? I was born in Sussex and brought up in St. Albans and moved back to Sussex when I was about six. The old man was based in the Navy up there, or so he said. I don't remember seeing a lot of water or ships up there. I'm 41, left school at sixteen and done ground works and road works. I've an older brother that's a Gooner.

Biggest rivals? Chelsea.

First game you ever went to? It was in 1972 when I was about 8 years old. My uncle Alan took me and it was an away game against Crystal Palace and resulted in a 2-2 draw. My second game was away to Southampton. I remember the next season '73, I went to the League Cup final against Norwich. From the age of 14 I'd use my paper round money to go to as many games as I could. I'd earn £3 a week and spend it all on football.

Memories of first game against rivals? I first saw Chelsea v Spurs on T.V. It was a two-legged Cup semi-final, and I remember I was in bed and the old man woke me up and let me watch the highlights. The first game I saw live was at White Hart Lane when we won 2-0, and that result relegated Chelsea. That day it was going off at both ends of the ground as Chelsea took a hell of a beating, in and off the pitch.

Finest team performance against them? Not in the last ten years. No, the F.A. Cup win at Stamford Bridge. It was the quarter finals and we won 3-2 with goals from Hazard, Archibald and Hoddle. Tottenham had a great support there that day and I remember a massive Spurs mob walking down the Kings Road from Sloane Square.

Best goal? The Hoddle goal in that Cup game. Hoddle done it for us all that season.

Worst defeat? The 6-1 defeat at the Lane. The Chelsea fans still sing about that to this day.

Biggest crowd? We had 78,000 against Sunderland in a Cup game and I remember a game at the Bridge when there were 66,000, but at the Lane against Chelsea there'd be about 60,000 there. They just let you in in them days, they crammed you in.

Best row, inside or outside the ground? I've seen plenty of scuffles and rows and people running up and down streets, but not a real good toe-to-toe row, not in the last few years anyway. When I get back in the pub though after the game there's always talk of "it went off here," or "it went off there." There's always trouble at the Chelsea games.

Have you ever been injured at a game, or nicked? I've been nicked at Spurs v Arsenal. There was a fight outside the club shop and about thirty Spurs fans were squaring up to this group of Arsenal. There was a bit of a stand off so silly bollocks here pushed me way to the front and I steams into them. Next minute I'm grabbed by two coppers. I wriggle free and get away and think I've had a result and got away with it, and then they pounced and I'm chucked into the back of a meat wagon. However, in court there was a mix up with the evidence from the Old Bill and the case was thrown out. I got a kicking up in Liverpool when I was 15 and still at school. We lost 3-1 and I was with a Spurs mob charging up the road after the Liverpool lot. We were at the back and two police vans pulled up and stopped the tail end of us from going any further. It didn't take long for the locals to suss out who we were. A bloke comes up to me and asked me the old chestnut "have you got the time mate?" I tried putting on my best Scouse accent but it didn't work. We bolted for it but I stood out like a sore thumb. I had on a donkey jacket with a big blue and white Spurs scarf tucked inside the collar. My mate got tripped up and they was on him like a pack of wolves. I couldn't leave him so I went back and I remember getting one punch in and then I was out, I was unconscious. I remember waking up getting to my feet. I was covered in blood and we staggered off up the road. Another mob of them came across the road. "Leave it out," I said, "we've just been done". They stopped and left us but they demanded my jacket. That was their game, the Scouse cunts, nicking ya clobber. A big mob came towards us that turned out to be our mob and as a bit of a piss take, and being one of the youngest there, they let me walk at the front of the firm all the way back to the station. I was as pleased as punch. All the shit you hear about how sporting the Liverpool fans are, is complete bollocks. They're fucking horrible robbing cunts. Ask any football fan what they really think of Liverpool supporters and most would say the same, one horrible bunch of cunts. The same day they were throwing darts at us and the geezer next to one got one in the shoulder. How sporting is that for fuck sake? It's a myth about them being fantastic fans.

What are your local Old Bill like? The Old Bill at Tottenham seems to be on first name terms with a lot of the faces. It if goes off they're straight there. You can't get away with a lot at Tottenham, they're clued up.

Name a player from their team you dislike or hate. Graeme Le Saux. I don't like his face, his make up, just the way he looks. He winds me up personally.

Your favourite all time player? Glen Hoddle. Some people might say Dave Mackay or Jimmy Greaves but I didn't really see them play so for me I'd go Glen Hoddle. He was world class and was England's Platini. If Hoddle had been French he would have won a hundred cups. People criticised his work rate but he didn't need to chase back. We had the likes of Roberts and Miller to do the defensive bit, just give him the ball and he could ping it anywhere. He's the best I've seen. His free kicks were going in every other week and he was a genius from set plays.

Have any of their managers, past or present, really got up your nose? Jose Mourinho for what he said about Spurs' performance at Chelsea recently. He said something along the lines that Spurs only come to defend and that they should have parked the team bus in front of their goal mouth.

The worst song or chant their fans sing? "He's Only a Poor Little Yiddo" and the chants "Yiddo". They don't bother us, we're proud of that nickname and sing Yid songs ourselves.

Your favourite song or chant about them? "Who the Fucking Hell Are You?" It's old and it's simple.

What's the furthest you've travelled to watch your team? Germany, and I've been out there twice for European games.

Are you a season ticket holder, and do you think your Club could do more for its fans? Yes I've had one for seven years. I think all supporters except say, Chelsea, would say their club could spend more on players, but maybe they could improve the public transport to the ground.

Have you ever worn a replica shirt? When I was a kid I wore the shirt and I was rossetted up with the bobble hat and knitted scarf. I never got cold and I would have a silk scarf tied around my wrist.

Have you ever cried at a game? Yes I have, at the Cup final replay against Man. City. I cried quietly, it was so emotional. At the first game I got nicked. I'd had a drink and a coach load of City came past and I done the wanker's sign at them and was arrested. They held me in the police cells until half-time when me and a City fan, who was also banged up, shared a taxi down to the stadium. When I got inside Glen Hoddle scored for us. What an eventful day.

Do you take your children to football? I've got six kids and five of them share a season ticket.

What would you do if a family member married a Rival? It wouldn't bother me, it don't matter.

Do you look out for any other teams' results?   Glasgow Rangers. It used to be Arsenal-Celtic, Tottenham-Rangers. I remember being at a game with me Gooner brother, Ricky, and he had an Arsenal-Celtic hat on and I had a Spurs-Rangers hat on and we danced arm in arm up the road singing "Brotherly Love". You should have seen the looks we got!

Are there any other teams you dislike?   Of course, Arsenal. That's not a normal game and it's got worse since the Sol Campbell episode. He held us to ransom. We could have got fifteen million for him from Man. Utd. The year before he left for nothing. I even spoke to him at a testimonial dinner and when I asked him if he would be going he just gave me a silly grin and said nothing. We've had other players like Stevie Walford and Willie Young and Pat Jennings go to Highbury, but Sol Campbell was different and I think he knew he was going to Arsenal. Money talks, a hundred grand a week would definitely talk, the greedy bastard.

If there's one player in the world, past or present, that you could sign, who would it be?   Steven Gerrard. He's the modern day complete footballer. He can tackle, pass and score goals.

If you had the choice of the National team winning the World Cup or your side winning the Premiership, which would you choose?   I'd be happy for Spurs to win the F.A. Cup before England won the World Cup.

Would you ground share with your rivals? Don't be silly, every club should have their own stadium. You can't share with other clubs can ya?"

PART THREE

NOTTINGHAM FOREST

 RIVALS

DERBY COUNTY

Name: **Wilmot**

Club: **Nottingham Forest**

We Mobbed Up At! I drove down from Burnley and met up with a few of Forests' finest. We had a few beers around the very trendy canal area and it turned into one good evening.

History/Honours? We've won everything, the European Cup twice, the League Cup, the Title. The Club's got a fantastic history.

Background? I come from Nottingham and I'm 41. I left school with a couple of qualifications, worked in a flour mill, then fucked off to Spain for a few years and lived with five girls from Reading in Loret de Mar. Happy days!

Biggest rivals? Derby County.

First game you ever went to?   Southampton away when I was still at school and two mini busloads of us went down to the Old Dell.

Memories of first game against rivals?   Brawling-wise it was probably the F.A. Cup game when Derby beat us 4-1. It was about 1981, Derby came onto the pitch and we tried to get on and have it with 'em.

Finest team performance against them?   I think it was the season we beat them 2-1 at their place and we had the likes of Ian Woam and Gary Charles in the side.

Best goal?   Any goal against them is a great goal.

Worst defeat?   The 4-1 defeat in the Cup.

Biggest crowd?   Thirty eight thousand at our place.

Best row, inside or outside the ground?   Derby's firm met up in a pub called The Sherbrooke Hotel, which is in the Meadows. We got wind of it and about 150 of us headed down there. We got there and a few of them were standing outside drinking, with the rest of them inside. They see us coming and ran inside and when we got to the pub it was trashed. The windows went in and the Derby lot inside went everywhere, over the bar, upstairs, out the back door, and we were climbing through the smashed windows to get at 'em. They tried to form an alliance with Leicester City, which came to fuck all.

Have you ever been injured at a game, or nicked?   No, I've not.

What are your local Old Bill like?   Very on top, dead organised, and like a row.

Name a player from their team you dislike or hate   Ted McMinn, 'is nickname was The Tinman when he was up at Rangers.

Your favourite all time player?   Stuart Pearce, he gave everything for Forest, just as he did for England.

Have any of their managers, past or present, really got up your nose?   Brian Clough, I was never really a big fan of his when he was at Forest.

The worst song or chant their fans sing?   The song every Club sings at us "We hate Nottingham Forest Over Land and Sea", etc. etc., and they call us Red Dogs and we call them Sheep Shaggers.

Your favourite song or chant about them?   We aint really got one but "We All Hate Rams and Rams and Rams" is sung often.

What's the furthest you've travelled to watch your team?   Probably Austria or Barcelona and I went out to Munich for the European Cup Final triumph.

Are you a season ticket holder, and do you think your Club could do more for its fans?   I'm currently banned for life so my chances of holding a season ticket are very slim.

Have you ever worn a replica shirt?   Never, not even on holiday or a wedding. No, never.

Have you ever cried at a game?   No, never.

Do you take your children to football?   I'm banned.

What would you do if a family member married a Rival?   It wouldn't bother me.

Are there any other teams you dislike?   Tottenham and
Sunderland because both sets of fans know me and hate me. I've
had a lot of trouble with Spurs. I went there by car once and we
left early while the game was still on and as we got back to the
car the police appeared and searched us. Anyway, a crowd gathered and they wanted our blood. The copper in charge started to
blame us because it looked like it was going to go off. I pointed
out to him that if he and his men hadn't of pulled us over and
gave us all the spill about names and where had we been, then
we would have been well away and out of the area. Things started to get worse as a mob of about a hundred Yids gathered at the
end of the road. "They know you're here", said the copper.
Things looked ugly so in the end, to diffuse the situation, the Old
Bill escorted us out of town.

**If there's one player in the world, past or present, that you
could sign, who would it be?**   Beckham present, Maradona
past.

**If you had the choice of the National team winning the World
Cup or your side winning the Premiership, which would you
choose?**   Forest to win the Premiership, although I'd love
England to win the World Cup.

Would you ground share with your rivals? Never, not in a million fucking years. It would never happen, although a few years
ago our Chairman was talking about sharing with Derby to help
pay towards the new stand, but it never happened. Thank fuck
for that. We might share with Notts. County, but never Derby.

Name: **Tommo**

Club: **Derby County**

We Mobbed Up At! I was due to meet Tommo in Derby prior to meeting the lads from nearby Nottingham, but due to work commitments he was forced to cancel. I'd heard about Tommo and how he was one of Derby County's main faces, from Boatsy, a Forest lad. Anyway, we managed to catch up with one another a week later and we spoke over the 'phone.

History/Honours? We won the F.A. Cup in 1946, we've won the old First Division a couple of times in the early 70s, and we were one of the original ten Clubs that founded the Football League. We used to play at the Baseball ground but have since moved to Pride Park, which, like a lot of these new stadiums, is somewhat out of town.

Background? I'm thirty nine, born in Derby inner city and left school with C.S.E.s in Maths, English, and Geography and when I left school I done Y.T.S.

Biggest rivals?   Nottingham Forest.

First game you ever went to?   It was at the Baseball ground in the late 70s. I was about 13 and went with my mate, K. At the time my older   brother was one of our main faces but these days he doesn't go at all and has no interest in football.

Memories of first game against rivals?   It was at Derby in the F.A. Cup and we won 2-0. About two hundred and fifty Forest came down Dairy House Road, which runs off of Cambridge Road, singing "Derby". We knew though that they weren't Derby and about 30 of us came in from the side of them, about another eighty came at them from the bottom of the road, and we backed them off and got the upper hand. At the final whistle we went onto the pitch and stormed across to where they were standing, and outside there was running battles all the way back into town. From then on I was hooked.

Finest team performance against them?   The 1983 F.A. Cup game that I've just described.

Best goal?   That's got to be last season when Paul Peshisolido had a hopeful shot at goal. It hit a plastic cup which had blown onto the pitch, and somehow the ball deflected into the net. Whether or not it would have gone in without the aid of the cup nobody knows. We went on to win 4-1 and the Club 'as kept the plastic cup and it's now in our trophy cabinet!

Worst defeat?   It normally ends in a draw, we rarely get beat by them.

Biggest crowd?   Thirty odd thousand in the F.A. Cup.

Best row, inside or outside the ground? The best row ever has got to again be, the F.A. Cup game at the Baseball ground. They don't always get it their own way, they have the bigger numbers but we always turn up.

Have you ever been injured at a game, or nicked? I've been nicked, probably around thirty times, and I got injured badly in a row at Barnsley. About a hundred of us went up there but didn't go into the game and afterwards we headed towards a social club where they were drinking. As we got there they came out and we clashed in the middle of the road. Their front line were well tooled up and squirted us with ammonia and gas, so we backed off. The Old Bill appeared and split it up and they escorted us back to the station, but we got out of the escort, went into their main pub, and they've followed us into the pub and mingled in with us. After about ten minutes our lot leave the pub and this Barnsley mob follow us out and it goes off again in the street. Barnsley shower us with bottles and glasses that they've bought out of the pub, and a pub further up the road empties out, and a mob of Barnsley Beer Monsters in their lumberjack check shirts and baggy tracksuit bottoms, pile into us. One of them is swinging a "for sale" sign above his head and I grab it and then someone wrestles it from me and smashes me over the head with it. The Bill have got hold of me and have said they're taking me to hospital but I said that I was all right and they could fuck off, so they nicked me. I'm covered in blood with a gaping wound in my head and gets taken off to the police station. About one o'clock in the morning I'm released without seeing a doctor or receiving any medical attention, and make my way to the railway station in a right state. I'm concussed and not quite sure where I'm going, and then a copper spots me and whisks me off to hospital in Sheffield where I'm kept in.

What are your local Old Bill like? Our copper, P.C. Britton, is one of the main spotters at England games and is part of the

N.C.I.S., and twelve of our lot were the first to get civil banning orders. We currently have two hundred and ninety fans on banning orders. I've just come off a ban but I heard through the grapevine that if I had of travelled to Portugal for the 2004 Euros, I would have been stopped from travelling, taken to court, and given another banning order. And we are supposed to be living in a free country!

Name a player from their team you dislike or hate. Stuart Pearce because he was Forest through and through.

Your favourite all time player? Bobby Davidson, he'd been to Leeds and played at Sheffield United and he was a real Roy of the Rovers player. He never stopped trying and he showed great spirit.

Have any of their managers, past or present, really got up your nose? Brian Clough. He done a lot for Derby but some of our fans see him as a bit of a traitor after he jumped ship.

The worst song or chant their fans sing? "When Derby go Down We Sing, We Sing, When Ian Bowyer Scores a Goal You Can Shove Your Hector up Your Hole".

Your favourite song or chant about them? "When You're Tired and Weary and Your Heart Will Miss a Beat, You Get Your Fucking Heads Kicked in as You Walk Down Shaftesbury Street. You Walk into the Popside and You Hear A Mighty Roar, Fuck Off You Forest Bastards, We Are the Derby Boys".

What's the furthest you've travelled to watch your team? Plymouth in the F.A. Cup. We took two hundred and fifty in a mob down there and we took the piss, running them everywhere in Union Street before the game. We gave the shout "D.L.F." (Derby Lunatic Fringe) and they bolted. There was no punches thrown, just one shout and they fucked off. After the game we came out onto the park beside the ground and one of their lot, who was way out in front of the rest of their mob, came into us waving a metal signpost about. He was quickly dispatched onto his arse and their lot turned and ran.

Are you a season ticket holder, and do you think your Club could do more for its fans?   No, I'm not a season ticket holder, and now that the Club has upped and moved to the new ground the atmosphere isn't the same. If you stand up, swear or sing you're automatically chucked out and banned so the spirit and the atmosphere are no longer there. Crowds lift the players and because of all this banning the life has been squeezed out of the Club. The fans are the heart of any Club; the blood supply to the players and you can't ban nearly three hundred fans, some for very flimsy reasons, and have the same atmosphere at the Club. I've heard it said so many times, but football is no longer a working class sport, football has become more like going to the opera at Derby. The old Baseball ground has been knocked down and is being re-developed with new houses, but to a lot of us the new ground is nothing like the old one. The Derby roar 'as long gone, plus the hooligans have moved their arena away from the ground and away from the city centre and away from the C.C.T.V. cameras. It doesn't often happen match days but it still goes on.

Have you ever worn a replica shirt?   No, it wouldn't suit my style.

Have you ever cried at a game?   It was when England played at Tottenham's White Hart Lane for a midweek international game. Eight Derby lads went into the packed Bank Pub on the High Street, words were exchanged with the Spurs' lads in there, and it kicks off. One of ours hits one of theirs, one of our lot is hit with a pool cue and five of our lot end up outside, with the other three trapped inside. As they rush back in, the door's pushed open and it hits the landlady on the nose and she's on the floor. The rest of the boys get out and they make their way up the road to another pub where there's thirty Derby drinking inside. A car then comes from behind, mounts the path scattering them everywhere, and the occupants of the car leap out and stab and slash at our lot with knives. Some are seriously wounded and lie moaning on the ground and a pool cue is smashed and broken over my head. The car then reverses off the pavement and drives off, they escape, no one is arrested, and our boys spent a week in hospital. I cry with both frustration and anger seeing my mates in such a state and it's not a nice feeling to see good mates stabbed. They just missed ones kidney, another was slashed with a machete all down his front, and another was slashed on the arm and across the throat. It's a wonder someone wasn't killed and we were only saved because a couple of the boys had seen what was going on and grabbed some gear off a nearby skip and come to the rescue.

Do you take your children to football?   No, they play football but if I was allowed back in I might take them.

What would you do if a family member married a Rival?   It would be someone to take the piss out of.

Do you look out for any other teams' results?   Yes West Ham, not because I like them but because I want them to stay in our division so we can play them. We went there in a league Cup match in a night game in the 80s. Two hundred and fifty of us gets off at Plaistow, we got into a pub and the Old Bill turn up and seal off the front of the pub, but we escape out of the back doors and head for the Queens Pub on Green Street. A few West Ham are standing outside drinking and we steam across the road at them, and they run back inside. We got on the march towards the ground and a few scuffles later we pile in through the doors of the Boelyn and clear it. A few West Ham front us outside the away end and make excuses about them not expecting us to turn up. Another team I watch out for is Millwall. We went there a few years back in a night game and about fifty of us found a pub near New Cross Gate. A kid then comes in and invites us up to a pub called The Rose. We know what to expect and one of our lot takes charge and leads us up the road. As the pub comes into view our main lad, Crossey, shouts "they're here" and a mob of Millwall stand in the street before us. An axe is thrown, along with a Kung Fu Star, at the pub doors, and the S.P.G. (Special Patrol Group) show up in vans and surround us. We're lead on a route march through all the narrow back streets and down to the ground as a large mob of menacing Millwall fans shadow our every move.

Are there any other teams you dislike?   Middlesborough. In the mid 80s we thought we were the top firm of the day and went up there in mini buses and settled in the Speedway Pub. It wasn't long before Boro found us and we came out of the pub to be faced by about sixty of them. We soon realised we'd been set up as another hundred appeared behind us. We were run back towards the pub, two of our lot were slashed across the arse, and our mob was in disarray. A lot of us tried to get over a spiked topped fence, but many were caught and beaten. A few of us found ourselves on a building site so we armed ourselves with bricks only for Boro to come around the corner carrying metal dustbin lids which, you've guessed it, they used as shields, just like gladiators. We were knackered having been well run ragged and ended up going across a cemetery and out onto a main road. The police turned up and for once we were grateful to see 'em and stood behind them for our own safety.

If there's one player in the world, past or present, that you could sign, who would it be?   Thierry Henry, he's pure entertainment.

If you had the choice of the National team winning the World Cup or your side winning the Premiership, which would you choose? England to win the World Cup. I've been to France where Birmingham and Derby had a row in Lille before the Colombia game.

Would you ground share with your rivals? No fucking way. Impossible, we hate the bastards.

PART FOUR

LEEDS UNITED

 RI V ALS

MANCHESTER UNITED

Name: **Dan Moore**

Club: **Leeds United**

We Mobbed Up At! I was introduced to Dan by my Barnsley connections and here he gives his insight into following Leeds.

History/Honours? Formed in 1904 as Leeds City, 1919 as Leeds United, turned professional in 1920, won League Cup in 1968, runners up in 1996, won League Division 1 in 1968-1969, 1973-1974, 1991-1992, runners up 1964-1965, '65-'66, '69-'70, '70-'71 and '71-'72. F.A. Cup winners 1972, runners up 1965, 1970 and 1973. F.A. Charity Shield 1969 and 1992. European Cup finalists 1972-1973. UEFA Cup runners up 1966-1967, winners 1967-1968 and 1970-1971.

Background? Born in Leeds, moved to Barnsley, currently living in Barnsley wanting a move back to Leeds.

Biggest rivals?   Man. Utd. – Scum.

First game you ever went to?   Can't remember but was told that my Dad took me as a baby.

Memories of first game against rivals?   The year we won the Title.

Finest team performance against them?   Any win against the dirty scum twats is great.

Best goal?   Jimmy Hasselbank, can't remember year, just remember busting my nose crowd surfing.

Worst defeat?   All defeats are hard to take against them.

Biggest crowd?   Sixty odd thousand at their place and about forty odd thousand at Elland Road.

Best row, inside or outside the ground?   We were at home to the scum and after a few drinks we headed down towards the ground. We couldn't get anywhere near them as the coppers had them in a tight escort and they were it seemed not too bothered about breaking away. A few scuffles broke out with their stragglers from the coach park, but nothing major. After the game, which we won 1-0 with a Harry Kewell goal, we joined the thousands of others waiting on the streets for them to come out of the away end. Everyone's up for it at this game, the scarfers, the granddads, everyone. A roar went up and everyone surged forward as United were let out onto the street. We were beaten back by coppers on horses, as bottles and bricks rained down on them and the pigs on horseback. It went on for a good half an hour with our lot being pushed back by the Old Bill and then regrouping. We were finally pushed over a footbridge which crosses the motorway, and ended up drinking in the Britannia Pub. We thought that was it and were a bit pissed off that we hadn't got to them when all of a sudden loads of Old Bill turned up and stood outside the front of the pub. We knew they must be near-by and forced our way out of the pub and sure enough as we got outside we were met with bottles and pots. We saw them opposite in a park, and charged. There was about forty of them and we got stuck into one another for a couple of minutes before the Old Bill arrived on horseback and broke it up. You can't fight a twat on a horse waving a bat above his head so it was time to scarper; it was hood up and head down.

Have you ever been injured at a game, or nicked? I got my jaw and cheekbone broken, and fractured my eye socket against W.B.A.

What are your local Old Bill like? Shit, they are like all others I suppose; they entice you into reacting to them.

Name a player from their team you dislike or hate. I fucking hate Roy Keane, for me he depicts the scum. Fucking good player though.

Your favourite all time player? My favourite has got to be Lucas Radebe; he is a soldier. Also loved Woodgate and Halfe Ingle Haaland.

Have any of their managers, past or present, really got up your nose? Ferguson, say no more, right twat.

The worst song or chant their fans sing? Can never hear them.

Your favourite song or chant about them? "Munich Air Disaster".

What's the furthest you've travelled to watch your team? Went to Barcelona the first time we got to the Champions' League (in recent years). Got beat 4-0 but had a top day.

Are you a season ticket holder, and do you think your Club could do more for its fans? I have been a season ticket holder since 1989-90 until mid 2002-03 season when I got banned. The Club should write to FCIOB to request a revoke on my banning order.

Have you ever worn a replica shirt? I only wear a replica shirt on my holidays.

Have you ever cried at a game? No.

Do you take your children to football? No, never.

What would you do if a family member married a Rival? I'd let them know where they stand.

Do you look out for any other teams' results? I quite like Doncaster.

Are there any other teams you dislike? Chelsea.

If there's one player in the world, past or present, that you could sign, who would it be? Ronaldo – at his best he is the best player in the world.

If you had the choice of the National team winning the World Cup or your side winning the Premiership, which would you choose? I would love to see both happen although finishing above Man. Utd. would be enough of a delight for me.

Would you ground share with your rivals? Not a fucking chance!

Name: **Michael Aronoffsky**
Club: **Manchester United**

We Mobbed Up At! I've known Mike for over twenty years. We both share a passion for Sumo wrestling. We speak to one another every week on the phone or by internet and here he tells me about his days following United.

History/Honours? We've won everything, the Premiership, F.A. Cups, Champions' League, the fucking lot, so put that in your pipes you jealous fuckers out there and smoke it. We're the top dogs in the whole of Europe.

Background? I've two sisters and family in Manchester. I was expelled from two schools and left with no qualifications, surprise, surprise! I have two beautiful daughters and I live and work in The States as a paramedic.

Biggest rivals?   Leeds United, they're fucking scum.

First game you ever went to?   Was probably about 35 years ago.

Memories of first game against rivals?   Was at Old Trafford in 1971.

Finest team performance against them?   Anytime we score against them and it shuts their dull fans right up.

Best goal?   Any Eric Cantona goal for Manchester United.

Worst defeat?   Can't remember, ha! ha!

Biggest crowd?   Probably between 66,000 and 67,000 at our place.

Best row, inside or outside the ground?   We've had many rows with them and I can't recall or have heard of, our lot coming unstuck against them once. However I have heard stories of them bullying fans with shirts on, and attacking families. How brave is that? One game that does come to mind was 1990 when I was standing at the forecourt at Old Trafford. It went toe to toe for ages and I didn't manage to get into the ground until the second half because it was going mental outside, and I'd rather miss the action on the field than where it really counts, out on the streets. You have to show the scum they can't come to Manchester and take liberties.

Have you ever been injured at a game, or nicked?   Yes, I've been hit by a bottle and needed stitches.

What are your local Old Bill like?   Same as anyone else's.

Name a player from their team you dislike or hate   David Batty.

Your favourite all time player?   Eric Cantona, a genius.

Have any of their managers, past or present, really got up your nose? Don Revie, a fucking twat.

The worst song or chant their fans sing?   "Marching on Together". What the fuck is that all about? They aint marching anywhere now their Club's skint. It couldn't happen to a nicer bunch of mongrels.

Your favourite song or chant about them?   Any song about them dossers is O.K. by me but "If you Follow Leeds You Must Be Scum" is a good 'un.

What's the furthest you've travelled to watch your team? Barcelona and California, U.S.A.

Are you a season ticket holder, and do you think your Club could do more for its fans?   Yes I still am and if I don't come over I let one of my family have my seat. I think the Club in general treats their fans fine. We have a fantastic stadium with probably the best facilities in the country.

Have you ever worn a replica shirt?   No.

Have you ever cried at a game?   Only tears of happiness when we win yet another trophy.

Do you take your children to football?   No, not any more.

What would you do if a family member married a Rival?   Kill 'em; it's as simple as that.

Do you look out for any other teams' results?   Yes, Chelsea. I've been to see them quite a few times when I was living in England and I know a lot of their boys who have always treated me well.

Are there any other teams you dislike?   Liverpool and Man. City. I hate the Scousers and I've just read that pile of shit by that nob jockey Nicho-arse Allt. Fuck me; he's got a vivid imagination! That's one of the worst Hoolie books I've ever read. Is he related to Porkie Brimson? He couldn't have written that because the Mickey Mousers can't read and write can they?

If there's one player in the world, past or present, that you could sign, who would it be?   Patrick Vierra, a world class player. I'd love him in a United shirt.

If you had the choice of the National team winning the World Cup or your side winning the Premiership, which would you choose?   United before England for me.

Would you ground share with your rivals?   Never, fuck that. I wouldn't share a thing with them.

PART FIVE

NEWCSTLE UNITED

RI**V**ALS

SUNDERLAND

Name: **Bonzo**

Club: **Newcastle United**

We Mobbed Up At! I met Ian in a coffee bar in Richmond, London. We met earlier through our mutual friend, Monty. Ian, besides his days at football has led, and still leads, a very colourful life. Say no more! This is what he said about the Geordie boys.

History/Honours? Not a lot in the last fifty years.

Background? Born and bred in the Newcastle area and today the M.D. of an international security and training organisation which provides various services to different areas in world security. I've followed Newcastle for 32 years.

Biggest rivals? The Macums (Sunderland).

First game you ever went to?   Wolves at home in 1972, it was the opening game of the season and we won 3-1.

Memories of first game against rivals?   It was away in the mid 70s in a Texaco Cup game at Joker Park. I can remember the score, we lost 2-1 and the violence still sticks in my mind, even though I was a twelve-year-old boy at the time.

Finest team performance against them?   1985 New Years Day and Peter Beardsley scored a hat trick.

Best goal?   Liam O'Brian at Joker Park in 1992 when he scored the best free kick I have ever seen. The goal won the game, which made it ten victories in a row, something they could never do.

Worst defeat? When we played the scum at home. We were losing 2-1 and Alan Shearer missed a penalty with just five minutes to go, something those sad bastards found highly amusing.

Biggest crowd? Due to the popular nature of this fixture tickets are like rocking horse shit for our end of the ground. It's the one game of the season everyone wants to go to but their end and their sections of the ground are never full.

Best row, inside or outside the ground?   There are so many that I could think of but one was when we totally smashed the fuck out of them. It was 1985 at Joker Park and 150 of us got tickets in their end. It was like a rat run as we smashed them everywhere and there was also running battles in different parts of the ground. We'd done our job in the Fullwell end and outside there were running battles going on. A question, which is raised amongst our lot, is why have they never come to our ground and had a proper go, and when we have made arrangements to meet them why do they never turn up? Could it be pre-fight nerves or a total lack of bottle? Let the readers of this book make their minds up. Could Sunderland run another firm? They couldn't run a fucking bath!

Have you ever been injured at a game, or nicked?   Yes, I got stabbed in the arm by Jocks at England v Scotland at Wembley Stadium in 1988.

What are your local Old Bill like?   It's the same throughout the U.K., the Old Bill are on top and seem to know the movements of all the key faces and players on the days of big games.

Name a player from their team you dislike or hate.   Gordon Armstrong, there are few words that could describe him. He was born less than a mile from St. James's Park and yet played for the scum and at every opportunity he had he would slag us off, the no good shithouse. Our fans fucking hate him. I wish him all the worst.

Your favourite all time player?   Malcolm McDonald.

Which manager, past or present, really got up your nose?   No, quite the opposite really. Sir Laurie McMenemy did a tremendous job taking those sad bastards down to the old Third Division where they belonged.

The worst song or chant their fans sing?   All of them, they are shit.

Your favourite song or chant about them? "We Fuckin' Hate Sunderland".

What's the furthest you've travelled to watch your team?   I've been all over Europe watching Newcastle in the Champions' League and the U.E.F.A. Cup.

Are you a season ticket holder, and do you think your Club could do more for its fans? No I'm not. The way Sir Bobby Robson was sacked was an absolute disgrace. Some people high up at Newcastle should take a good look at themselves before passing judgement on other people.

Have you ever worn a replica shirt? Never.

Have you ever cried at a game? Italy, when Chris Waddle missed a penalty for England.

Do you take your children to football? My eldest son is a season ticket holder.

What would you do if a family member married a Rival? Cut their fucking heads off.

Do you look out for any other teams' results? Yes, Newcastle United's reserves, I'm Newcastle through and through.

Are there any other teams you dislike? There is a very small team from North Yorkshire who have their moments now and then but other than them, none.

If there's one player in the world, past or present, that you could sign, who would it be? Thierry Henry, world class.

If you had the choice of the National team winning the World Cup or your side winning the Premiership, which would you choose? It would be Newcastle winning the Premiership.

Would you ground share with your rivals? No, it would not make sense. Newcastle are in the Premier League so Sunderland would be better off sharing with Blyth Spartans as they would have a similar fan base and the financial restraint would be the same.

Name: **Randolph Campbell**

Club: **Sunderland A.F.C.**

We Mobbed Up At! I met Randolph up in Barnsley at the K.G.B. Bar.

History/Honours? 2 F.A. Cups 1937 and 1973 and numerous League Championships. Used to be at Roker Park then moved to the 48,000 all seater Stadium of Light.

Background? You don't need to know.

Biggest rivals? Scum United, black and white twats.

First game you ever went to? Norwich City at Roker Park.

Memories of first game against rivals? Getting beat 3-1 at St. James Park.

Finest team performance against them?   The play offs, winning 2-0 at St. James Park.

Best goal?   Marco Gabbiadini in the play offs at St. James Park.

Worst defeat?   Any against the Geordie wankers.

Biggest crowd?   Full house at The Stadium of Light – 48,000.

Best row, inside or outside the ground?   Glasgow Rangers were at it all day in Sunderland. Newcastle they are always up for it, all outside.

Have you ever been injured at a game, or nicked?   Got nicked fighting Boro outside Roker Park in 1995. Worst injuries have been a broken nose and the odd black eye.

What are your local Old Bill like?   Ass holes, they are all Geordie wankers.

Name a player from their team you dislike or hate.   Alan Shearer, a tosser.

Your favourite all time player?   Kevin Ball, 'cos he gave it his all in every game and wore his shirt with pride.

Have any of their managers, past or present, really got up your nose?
Kevin Keegan when he thought they had the right to win the Premier League.

The worst song or chant their fans sing?   All of them 'cos they sing them!

Your favourite song or chant about them?   "With an N and an

E and a W.C. an A and an S and TLE United, Newcastle United
Fuck Off, Fuck Right Off you Black and White Cunts".

What's the furthest you've travelled to watch your team?
Plymouth.

**Are you a season ticket holder, and do you think your Club
could do more for its fans?**   Used to be at Roker Park, but
banned at the moment.

Have you ever worn a replica shirt?   Yes, I buy a home and
away shirt every time to wear at work or just dossing round the
house.

Have you ever cried at a game?   Yes, when we got relegated
against Gillingham.

Do you take your children to football?   No, he's not old
enough.

What would you do if a family member married a Rival?   It
would never happen, at least I hope not.

Do you look out for any other teams' results?   Barnsley, 'cos I
now live there, and Glasgow Rangers.

Are there any other teams you dislike?   Middlesborough.

**If there's one player in the world, past or present, that you
could sign, who would it be?**   Maradona – pure genius.

**If you had the choice of the National team winning the World
Cup or your side winning the Premiership, which would you
choose?**   No choice – Sunderland winning the Premier League.

Would you ground share with your rivals? Fuck that, I would rather die first.

PART SIX

W O L V E S

R I   A L S

WEST BROMWICH ALBION

Name: **Abbo**

Club: **Wolverhampton Wanderers**

We Mobbed Up At! Abbo's abode, during his lunch break. I know Abbo through Gilly and the Wolves mob. He's one of their top boys and can tell a good tale. Here's what he had to say.

History/Honours? The League Cup and Sherpa Van, E.U.F.A. Cup, finalists against Spurs, the old First Division winners, three or four times. F.A. Cup winners. We've won everything domestically over the years.

Background? I was born in Wensbury in the borough of West Bromwich 38 years ago. I left school with 'O' levels in Art, Chemistry, Biology, English Literature, Geography, and Geology. I've three brothers who all follow Wolves. My first job was as a hairdresser and I'm now a floor layer, but in between I was a transport manager.

Biggest rivals?   West Bromwich Albion, the shit. We're just six miles apart and it's not just a dislike for them, it's a real hatred.

First game you ever went to?   1971 when I was six. It was a Texaco Cup game and I went with the old man.

Memories of first game against rivals?   I must have been about 12 or 13 and it was a glorious, hot, sunny day. It kicked off in the street and one of our lads set fire to the grass bank outside. It quickly spread to a part of the stands and the whole lot went up.

Finest team performance against them?   It has a very small bearing on me what happens on the field but when we beat them 3-2 up there when Steve Bull and Andy Mutch scored, that was a good result.

Best goal?   A 93rd minute equaliser in extra time. It had been raining for two days and we were drowning wet and the ball came over as we were getting ready to leave and it was in the back of the net. We went fucking mad.

Worst defeat?   When they beat us I think, 3-1, and our goal-keeper got involved and we had them under siege for two hours and the Old Bill kept them in until they'd cleared the surrounding streets of Molineax.

Biggest crowd?   Forty three thousand when our ground had the old terraces.

Best row, inside or outside the ground?   They never turn up but the best one was outside Moonies Pub. They got off a bus near Sainsburys and they'd been threatening to come over for hours and then they suddenly appeared just before kick off. A shout in the pub went up that "they're here" so we went onto the street, turned left near the library, no Old Bill, and there they was. One of their lot was a mouthy bird who was well game, but she got knocked out and they soon scattered.

Have you ever been injured at a game, or nicked? I got nicked at Port Vale and stabbed in the shoulder by a West Ham firm. Some ginger cunt with a ponytail came through the parked cars and coaches, broke a glass on the wall and stabbed me. The rest of our lot were rucking with them before the game, all the way down from Plaistow. People were coming out of houses and joining in, and men doing roadside repairs on cars used their spanners as weapons and joined in. A man pulled up at the lights with a baby on his lap and his wife driving. He saw the action and dumped the kid on his wife's lap and shouts "come on you cunts", leaps from the car and joins in.

What are your local Old Bill like? Ask any football firm in the country what the West Midlands Old Bill are like. It's full riot gear and the operational support unit seem to love confrontation. Enough said.

Name a player from their team you dislike or hate. Lee Hughes a ginger little ….. Where he is now is the best place for him.

Your favourite all time player? Steve Bull, he's a legend and was so loyal to the Club. He could have made a big money move but he stayed with the Club and that would be unheard of these days. Also, it gave us the chance to cheer on one of our players in an England shirt.

Have any of their managers, past or present, really got up your nose? Brian Talbot, he'd be up and down the touchline.

The worst song or chant their fans sing? "Slap a Dingle", but they've got some front. They were voted the worst dressed supporters in the country by a football magazine and they have no class.

Your favourite song or chant about them? To be honest we don't really sing at them. That aint our bag, we just insult them.

What's the furthest you've travelled to watch your team? Flying to Newcastle and watching us win 4-1. I've been to Carlisle, Wrexham, Cardiff, Plymouth, all the far- flung places.

Are you a season ticket holder, and do you think your Club could do more for its fans? No, not at the moment. Cheaper prices and maybe bring the pitch nearer the stands, you're too far away. I'd sometimes go to away games and players looked different to me and then I realised it was because at home I couldn't see 'em because they were that far away.

Have you ever worn a replica shirt? No, never. As a kid my mum and dad bought me a Wolves' kit when I was seven or eight.

Have you ever cried at a game? I've been close to it as football can be very emotional. When we won the play-offs at Cardiff I was close and when we won the Sherpa Van Trophy and the players came to our end of the stadium at the end, it was hard to hold back the tears.

Do you take your children to football? I do and if I take the kids it's not the same as going with the lads when it's straight in the ground and swerve the pub.

What would you do if a family member married a Rival? Disown them.

Do you look out for any other teams' results? Glasgow Rangers.

Are there any other teams you dislike?   Birmingham, we thought they were something for years. We've done them twice and broke the back of them, we finished them, we've slaughtered them twice, we battered them. They know we done them, it was all their boys. Also Tranmere who we've had a thing with, stemming from England games. One of their boys wanted to fight Gilly one on one and Gilly knocked him out and put him to sleep for two days. It were mental.

If there's one player in the world, past or present, that you could sign, who would it be?   George Best, a genius, a fucking genius.

If you had the choice of the National team winning the World Cup or your side winning the Premiership, which would you choose?   England to win the World Cup as any Club can win the Premiership, especially if you have the money.

Would you ground share with your rivals?   Over my dead body. If we'd shared with West Brom. I'd never go again, it just wouldn't fucking happen, believe me.

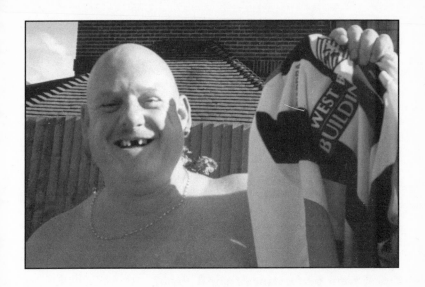

Name: **The Belly**

Club: **West Bromwich Albion**

We Mobbed Up At! The Green Dragon in Darliston. It was a lovely sunny Friday afternoon and the pub was buzzing. Gilly sat in the corner listening intently as he munched on his packet of pork scratchings, washed down with lashings of Babycham and sweet sherry.

History/Honours? '69, we won the F.A. Cup with a Jeff Astle goal against Everton, and various promotions.

Background? I was born in Darliston 41 years ago, left school on a Wednesday and started work on the Monday as a stores operative. I lost my brother sixteen years ago who was a big Albion fan. The area I come from is ninety five per cent Wolves fans.

Biggest rivals? Wolves.

First game you ever went to? When I was about eight or nine my auntie took me and our kid.

Memories of first game against rivals? When I was still at school. I was about fourteen or fifteen and me and my brother got separated from the rest of the Albion fans and got chased from the Molineaux all the way back to Bilston. We were stopped by some big blokes who were about forty years of age and asked if we were Albion fans. "No" we replied. "Well, who's the Wolves' goal keeper?" they asked and we couldn't answer. I pulled out a penknife from me pocket and jabbed it towards them. "First one near us gets this," I said, and they backed off. That was my first memory of playing them.

Finest team performance against them? At the Hawthorns, it was one a piece and Bob Taylor made it 2-1 with a diving header.

Best goal? Darren Bradley's goal from just over the halfway line. He hit it and it went in, a wonderful goal.

Worst defeat? There's never really been big margins, it's always the odd goal in it. Anyway, when we lose I tend to forget it.

Biggest crowd? The Albion at the moment holds about twenty eight thousand. I've been to Molineaux when there's been forty odd thousand packed in there and I've also been there when they've had seven thousand. In the lower league they had three and a half thousand there once when they played Hull City, and every Wolves' fan I've ever spoken to claims to have been at that game. There must have been two hundred thousand hiding somewhere there. We took a banner to the next Derby game with "where were you against Hull City?" and the Old Bill made us take it down.

Best row, inside or outside the ground?   I've been in the Northbank with about ten mates, which in those days was the done thing, to go into the home supporters' end and try to take it. We shouted "Albion" and jumped out onto the pitch and back around to our end. Fair play to Wolves, they always turn out for us. You've got to give it to them, they give us three thousand two hundred tickets at their place and all of our lot are the boys, no women and children, just all boys. You can feel the hatred.

Have you ever been injured at a game, or nicked?   I've been nicked a few times but never been injured.

What are your local Old Bill like?   You've got no chance and if it goes off they're on your case. I was once set up by them. It was going off outside the station and our liaisons officer pointed out a Wolves fan who'd somehow got mixed in with us. "Go and hit him," said the copper, like he was my best mate. I looked at him and said, "do you think I'm stupid?". He shrugged his shoulders and laughed. That's how far they will go, they love it, double time on a Sunday, and they're the winners.

Name a player from their team you dislike or hate   He's left now but that Keith Curle was a hard bastard and arrogant. I did like and respect Steve Bull as he stayed loyal and I admire him for that.

Your favourite all time player?   Bob Taylor, he turned out to be a bargain buy.

Have any of their managers, past or present, really got up your nose?   Yes, there's two, Mark McGee and Dave Jones who looks shifty with them eyes.

The worst song or chant their fans sing?   "Tesco Carrier Bag" because of the team shirt we wear.

Your favourite song or chant about them?   "Slap a dingle".
What's the furthest you've travelled to watch your team?
Carlisle United.

Are you a season ticket holder and do you think your Club could do more for its fans?   I've been one for the last three or four years and they've still kept the kids for a quid, which is great.

Have you ever worn a replica shirt?   Oh aye, I wear one all the time. If I came in here on a Saturday night and the dingles had lost and I walked in with an Albion shirt on, it could turn a bit nasty. You've got to know when and where to wear your colours.

Have you ever cried at a game?   I've cried for me brother, just wishing he were here to see Albion gain promotion and play in the Premiership and enjoy some success. I always think of him.

Do you take your children to football?   Yes I do. They're season ticket holders and they keep me out of trouble, plus it's a lot safer these days inside the grounds. I know where to take them and where not to take 'em. The trouble is still there but you have to know how to avoid it.

What would you do if a family member married a Rival?
Disown them.

Do you look out for any other teams' results?   Walsall. Years ago I'd go to Albion one week and Walsall the next, and I look out for Darlo our local non-league side.

Are there any other teams you dislike?   Everybody used to hate Man. Utd. but I read in the paper this week that it's Chelsea that's taken over United's mantle of English Footballs Most Hated Side. I think that's right with the obscene amounts of money they've spent. It's ruined football.

If there's one player in the world, past or present, that you could sign, who would it be?   Pele, he was superb and he would have looked good in an Albion Shirt.

If you had the choice of the National team winning the World Cup or your side winning the Premiership, which would you choose? West Brom. winning the Premiership.

Would you ground share with your rivals? No, you couldn't do it. We'd smash the facilities and the ground to pieces and they'd do likewise if they shared the Hawthorns.

PART SEVEN

CHESTERFIELD

 RI V ALS

MANSFIELD TOWN

Name: **Choco**

Club: **Chesterfield**

We Mobbed Up At! I was given Choco's name and number by my Forest, Mansfield and Derby County connections. They told me "if you want to know anything about the Spireites then Choco's ya man". Here's what he told me about his football going days.

History/Honours? Various promotions and championships and we reached the semis of the F.A. Cup in '97 where we lost to Middlesborough in a replay after drawing 3-3 at Old Trafford in the first game.

Background? Born in Chesterfield 39 years ago. I left school with no qualifications and worked in an abattoir for twelve years. I'm currently working as a painter and decorator.

Biggest rivals?   Mansfield Town.

First game you ever went to?   Man. Utd. v Porto in the 70s. I went with my step-dad who was a United fan.

Memories of first game against rivals?   When I was about 15 I remember Mansfield coming over on double decker buses. It used to kick off and I'd stand there watching it.

Finest team performance against them?   We beat them 3-1 about four years ago and took about three and a half thousand fans over there.

Best goal?   Any goal is a good goal against them.

Worst defeat?   Any defeat is hard to swallow against them.

Biggest crowd?   About nine and a half thousand and the place would be packed.

Best row, inside or outside the ground?   Man. City were play-ing at Mansfield and forty of us decided to go over there. We steamed into Mansfield's mob and the Man. City lads joined in and we chased them everywhere. They didn't stand and fight and that day we humiliated them.

Have you ever been injured at a game, or nicked?   I got a bad beating and put in hospital at Rotherham. Five of us didn't go in and we were walking up towards the ground when the final whistle went. Thousands of them came pouring out and it ended up with us getting a good kicking.

What are your local Old Bill like?   One of the boys that used to go with our mob is now a detective in the police. We have pho-tos of him and this has given him the right hump.

Name a player from their team you dislike or hate.   All of them, they're all scabs the fucking lot of them.

Your favourite all time player?   Alan Birch. He was a midfield player who was skilful and could score goals. Danny Wilson and Jeff Salmon were also good around that time.

Have any of their managers, past or present, really got up your nose? No matter who was in charge I'd hate him because he was Mansfield's manager.

The worst song or chant their fans sing?   That fucking daft chanting of "Yellow, Yellow". It's so fucking annoying.

Your favourite song or chant about them?   "Chim Chimney, Chim Chimney Charoo We Hate Those Bastards in Yellow and Blue".

What's the furthest you've travelled to watch your team? Torquay on a Wednesday night in November and twenty four of us went, and Carlisle on a Tuesday night when we took about a hundred up there.

Are you a season ticket holder, and do you think your Club could do more for its fans? No, never had a season ticket and the club's got no money because one of the former Chairmen ploughed money into his ice-hockey club.

Have you ever worn a replica shirt? I've worn a replica shirt to England games in the Euro 2004 out in Portugal.

Have you ever cried at a game?   When we played Boro it was very emotional. We were two nil up then went three two down and then we equalised, but got hammered in the replay.

Do you take your children to football? They play football and
sometimes they come to watch games.

What would you do if a family member married a Rival? No
way would I let that happen. My ex father in law lost his house
through the miners' strike and while them scabs in
Nottinghamshire carried on working, families around here
struggled to make ends meet. No, it runs far too deep to let a
scab into my family. Some people lost everything because of the
strike and some people never recovered. This issue is more
important than football.

Do you look out for any other teams' results? Man. Utd. I
remember the days of Pearson and Greenoff.

Are there any other teams you dislike? Yea, Mansfield
Reserves, Sheffield Wednesday, Sheffield United, and Leeds.

**If there's one player in the world, past or present, that you
could sign, who would it be?** Maradona. The way he is now is
not the way he used to be plus we'd be well all right for the
Charlie!

**If you had the choice of the National team winning the World
Cup or your side winning the Premiership, which would you
choose?** I'd pick Chesterfield to win the Premiership, it's club
before country for me.

Would you ground share with your rivals? I hate 'em, no way,
the whole town hates them. They're twenty mile away but that's
not far enough in my book. I wished they'd come into
Chesterfield more often for a drink so we could sort them out.
It's pure hatred and its what rivalry is all about.

Name: **Palmer**

Club: **Mansfield Town**

We Mobbed Up At! In a bar down near the canal in Nottingham, and he claims to be Britain's most handsome hooligan!

History/Honours? European Cup 1997, no not really. Various promotions but nothing to speak of.

Background? I'm 34 and come from Mansfield and my dad and brother are keen football fans.

Biggest rivals? The scumbag Chesterfield Spireites.

First game you ever went to? 1977 against Stoke City when they invaded the pitch and took the piss.

Memories of first game against rivals?   I was 17 and about 50 of us went on a coach to Chesterfield and I was arrested after five minutes of being on the streets.

Finest team performance against them?   They usually beat us, but I do remember one 2-0 win.

Best goal?   Paul Holland, he scored from the halfway line, he hit it and it went in the top corner.

Worst defeat?   Losing 5-4 to them in a play-off game.

Biggest crowd?   79,000, no I'm only joking I mean, nine and a half thousand at Mansfield!

Best row, inside or outside the ground?   Two years ago, two hundred of us left their ground at half time and went straight into their end. They held us off and they were as game as fuck and it went on for a good five minutes.

Have you ever been injured at a game, or nicked?   Lincoln City who've got a good little mob. They turned up about a hundred strong, but split into different mobs. We clashed with their Irish gypsy mob and we went at them with pool cues and bottles. When they realised they were being chased by five of us, they turned and give it to us. I got side-winded and two of ours got stabbed.

What are your local Old Bill like?   Same Old Bill as Forest Old Bill, wankers.

Name a player from their team you dislike or hate   Simon Coleman, he went to Chesterfield from Mansfield. The long streak of piss.

Your favourite all time player?   Rod Arnold our goalkeeper, a great keeper.

Have any of their managers, past or present, really got up your nose?   John Duncan when he got them to the semis of the F.A. Cup. Thank God they lost.

The worst song or chant their fans sing?   "Scabs" it's all to do with the miners' strike, but when we play them all the old miners turn out.

Your favourite song or chant about them?   "He's only a Poor Little Spireites, His Face is all Tattered and Torn, He Made Me Feel Sick So I Hit Him With a Brick, and Now he Don't Sing Any More".

What's the furthest you've travelled to watch your team? Carlisle.

Are you a season ticket holder, and do you think your Club could do more for its fans?   Yea, let the banned fans in, they seem to ban anyone these days. I'm on a ban and they're now taking me to the Civil courts for another ban.

Have you ever worn a replica shirt?   Yea, I have on holiday.

Have you ever cried at a game?   Yea, when I got smashed on the nose.

Do you take your children to football?   If I could get in I would take them, but because I'm banned I would 'ave to wait outside for 'em.

What would you do if a family member married a Rival? Disown them.

Do you look out for any other teams' results? Forest and Notts. County and Newcastle. Although County hate us we don't mind them. I also have a soft spot for Chelsea.

Are there any other teams you dislike? Obviously Derby and Lincoln City, Sunderland, and Tottenham.

If there's one player in the world, past or present, that you could sign, who would it be? Alan Shearer, a great player.

If you had the choice of the National team winning the World Cup or your side winning the Premiership, which would you choose? England to win the World Cup. Mansfield would never in my lifetime win the Premiership, not even if some Russian billionaire or some Jewish geezer ploughed millions into the Club.

Would you ground share with your rivals? No chance because we fucking hate 'em. We'd smash their faces in every week.

PART EIGHT

F U L H A M

R I V A L S

Q U E E N S   P A R K   R A N G E R S

Name: **Barry (Larry) Lawrence**

Club: **Fulham**

We Mobbed Up At! Larry dropped by the King estate, which is nestled between the rolling Sussex Downs and the inviting waters of the English Channel. Over tea and biscuits we discussed Larry's love of Fulham, his love life and more.

History/Honours? Founded in 1879 as Fulham St. Andrews, which was a church team and went into the football league in 1907. We've been in the semi-finals five times and the F.A. Cup final once, in 1975, when we lost to West Ham 2-0.

Background? I was born in Parsons Green, brought up around Fulham and moved to Hounslow in West London when I was about seven. I lived on the Beavers Estate and my first job on leaving school was installing double glazing on the estate. I'm currently a successful, self-employed businessman.

Biggest rivals?   Queens Park Rangers.

First game you ever went to?   The F.A. Cup games, the year we got to the final. I remember watching us against Forest and Carlisle when I was nine years old. I went with me dad, me uncles and me good mate, Paul Nash, whose family were all Orient supporters but he came over with us lot to Fulham. We played about fourteen games that year after replays to get to the final.

Memories of first game against rivals?   One memory was an F.A. Cup match at Craven Cottage. It was 1981-1982 and we beat them 2-0. I think Gordon Davies got one of the goals.

Finest team performance against them?   There's not normally a lot in it between the two sides. It would always seem to end in a draw or a win by the odd goal. But the 2-0 Cup win was a great result and the atmosphere was electric.

Best goal?   Any goal is good enough against them.

Worst defeat?   There's never been a 4-0 or 5-0 and as I say, it's always the odd goal that decides it.

Biggest crowd? Probably about twenty two thousand at Craven Cottage.

Best row, inside or outside the ground?   It normally kicks off around Hammersmith Broadway. If we play over there the two groups normally clash around Hammersmith, which is situated between the two grounds. The two clubs are only about three miles apart. One year at Craven Cottage the Rangers fans were fighting amongst themselves and outside, their midget leader, with the 70s haircut and the gold teeth, was running around like a man possessed trying to rally his troops.

Have you ever been injured at a game, or nicked? Yea I've been nicked. It was against Carlisle United at Craven Cottage. The final whistle went and their lot ran onto the pitch from behind the goal so about sixty of us ran on and went towards them. They've bottled it and run back onto the terraces. I've stopped and picked up a handful of mud, shaped it into a ball and hurled it towards the Carlisle firm. "Whack", it hit one of them right in the boat race. "Shot" I shouted and the crowd in front of me parted as the police came bustling through, grabbed me and marched me off. I received a £50 fine for my spot of cricket practice.

What are your local Old Bill like? They're good at catching people throwing mud balls! No, they're just normal; same as anywhere else.

Name a player from their team you dislike or hate.   Stan Bowles or Rodney Marsh. They were good players but flash bastards.

Your favourite all time player? Not my era but all the old boys rave on about Johnny Haynes, but I'd say Gordon Davies. He was a prolific goal scorer for Fulham and I think we paid about £5,000 for him from somewhere like Merthyr Tydfil. He was once a schoolteacher.

Have any of their managers, past or present, really got up your nose?   All their managers have been faceless; they've had some right shit managers.

The worst song or chant their fans sing?   "Rangers, Rangers" and "Come on you Rs". They don't really sing a lot about us because they have trouble stringing two words together.

Your favourite song or chant about them? Any song that slags off Rangers.

What's the furthest you've travelled to watch your team?
Craven Cottage. No, not really! I went up to Carlisle with Paul
Nash and Paul Nye, me two mates who I went with to most
games.

**Are you a season ticket holder, and do you think your Club
could do more for its fans?** I have had a season ticket but not at
the moment. I think the club could do more for its fans by perhaps winning a few more games and scoring a few more goals.

Have you ever worn a replica shirt? Yes.

Have you ever cried at a game? Yea, at the '75 Cup final when
we lost. I was ten and went with all the family and was gutted.
All the build up and we turned up in our colours with the big
top hats on and scarves, and we got beat. I was devastated but it
didn't stop us having a big party back at Fulham.

Do you take your children to football? She's too young at the
moment but I will when she's older.

What would you do if a family member married a Rival? It
wouldn't bother me. There'd be a bit of banter but nothing serious.

Do you look out for any other teams' results? Not Chelsea.
Arsenal because me brother, the black sheep of the family, supports them. Barnet, because I've got cousins up there. Raith
Rovers, because it's always been a joke between me dad and me
uncle. When the results came on on Saturdays they'd laugh and
say "they lost again".

Are there any other teams you dislike? A lot of Fulham fans
don't like Chelsea, but like most other football fans I can't stand
Man. Utd.

If there's one player in the world, past or present, that you could sign, who would it be?   On his day and in his prime, Maradona. He was a special player.

If you had the choice of the National team winning the World Cup or your side winning the Premiership, which would you choose?   I take Fulham to win the Premiership because I don't think England have any chance of winning the World Cup. Come to think of it I don't think we've got any chance of winning the Premiership.

Would you ground share with your rivals?   We've ground shared with Rangers but going by attendances we were about four thousand down on the gate. It seems that other clubs are laughing at ya because you can't afford to have ya own ground. I can't work out why we moved in the first place. Sharing aint a good thing for clubs.

Name: **Gregor**

Club: **Queens Park Rangers**

We Mobbed Up At! Me, Fat Pat, Ginger Bob, and the Para met up with Gregor on Shepherds Bush Green where we had a few beers and talked about the old days. Gregor had some great stories to tell and had us in stitches! He's well known at nearly every Club in the Country and is the first to admit that he loves a row, and for a little fella he's as game as fuck.

History/Honours? We beat W.B.A. in the League Cup final in 1967. We finished runners up in the old first division under Dave Sexton in 1976, and lost the F.A. Cup Final to the Yids.

Background? Born in Notting Hill. I'm now 43 years old and went to school at Isaac Newton, now and again, in Ladbrooke Grove. I left school and went labouring on various building sites.

Biggest rivals? Fulham, but Rangers have a thing with Luton, Oxford, Norwich, and Forest.

First game you ever went to? Burnley when I was about 13 if I remember correctly, and both sides needed the points to win the league. I went on my own as a sightseer and that's when I first got involved. I remember jumping on a big geezer's back as it all kicked off.

Memories of first game against rivals? The Fulham Q.P.R. thing was more to do with areas that football. We used to mob up and march down there and go straight in the Thames Bank, which was their end. As we queued up to get in we could see all their boys waiting at the top of the terraces. We'd split up and some would go straight up towards them and others would go around the back and work their way into the middle. A big gap would open up and off it went. One time we ran them out of their end five times, but they kept coming back. The late 70s was the first Rangers-Fulham game I went to and we always took a top mob to Fulham. We had the top boys, the C. mob that drunk in the Vic, the Ladbrooke Grove boys, the Northolt boys. We were a solid mob when we went to Fulham.

Finest team performance against them? I missed most of the football because I was either arrested or thrown out.

Best goal? Either a Rodney Marsh or a Stan Bowles special.

Worst defeat? No, nothing that sticks in my mind

Biggest crowd? About 25,000.

Best row, inside or outside the ground? We went in their end one year and backed them right off, then into the gap that opened up appeared loads of Chelsea boys. Next minute they were everywhere, they were massive and ran us all over the place. Outside, the Chelsea boys were waiting for us and a few of our boys knew some of them and the rest of us just swerved it. At the time Chelsea wasn't a lot of our boys' favourite team. Nowadays most of us get along fine, although certain parts of our crowd sing songs about Chelsea.

Have you ever been injured at a game, or nicked?   I'd had a serious car crash and was let out for the day so I went over to see what was going on at Fulham and Sheffield United. I'd been in hospital for nine months and a row has kicked off outside the ground. I fell over, went back to the hospital and after three days they discovered I'd broken my leg again. I have been nicked against Fulham.

What are your local Old Bill like?   Two faced, you have your good days and your bad days, like most Old Bill.

Name a player from their team you dislike or hate   No-one really. They used to chop and change so much I didn't really know who was in their side and I didn't care.

Your favourite all time player?   Rodney Marsh, Stan Bowles or Dave Thomas, any one of them three.

Have any of their managers, past or present, really got up your nose?   Kevin Keegan, I didn't really like him, he's a Scouser.

The worst song or chant their fans sing?   Never heard them sing.

Your favourite song or chant about them?   There isn't one. Our fans are more inclined to sing about Chelsea.

What's the furthest you've travelled to watch your team?   Liverpool in 1976, which was the year we nearly won the league.

Are you a season ticket holder, and do you think your Club could do more for its fans?   The Club could do more for the youngsters in the area, maybe get a few more young kids coming through the ranks and getting into the First team. Me and a season ticket? You're joking!

Have you ever worn a replica shirt?   No.

Have you ever cried at a game?   In frustration when we lost to Spurs in the F.A. Cup Final replay. I was gutted.

Do you take your children to football?   Yes sometimes, but you have to choose your games and know where to go and what, and what not to do, if you get my drift.

What would you do if a family member married a Rival?   It wouldn't bother me as long as they were sensible.

Do you look out for any other teams' results?   I just look out for the results in general but I like to see how Millwall and Chelsea have got on.

Are there any other teams you dislike?   I hate Oxford because they think they're the bollocks. Every time we've gone there we've done their mob but they never admit it, they never give us credit. We had a row, twenty of us and a hundred of them, and me and one of their black fellas were rucking and I got arrested on the forecourt of McDonalds. Luton and us we just hate one another, and it's been going on for years. Ten of us ran 60 of them Migs out of our seats. I was watching a documentary on T.V. one night and it was on C.C.T.V. footage of our lot rowing with Luton on a station platform. What made me laugh was a well-known Chelsea face, who's rather on the large side, was wobbling up the platform! Norwich is another team we've had some blinding rows with. Norwich was another team that would turn out in numbers for us. Every time we played them there'd be two or three hundred of them and it would be like World War Three. We plotted up in a pub up there and a few of our young lot, accompanied by Fat Pat from Chelsea who was guesting with us for the day, decided to go and have a scout around. They turned the corner and within seconds they were running back breathless, "they're here, they're here!". We came storming out the pub and three hundred of them came straight into us, it went mental. Another time one of their boys put me on me arse outside Argos as we came out of the train station. A copper saw him, grabbed him, and because it was going off all over the place, he handcuffed him to some railings and shot off up the road to break up more fighting. One of my mates noticed this and said, "here, there's that geezer that knocked you out". Five of us gave him a good kicking and as he tried to get away he pulled the railings away. He couldn't escape, he was fucked.

If there's one player in the world, past or present, you could sign who would it be?   George Best or Nedved.

If you had the choice of the National team winning the World Cup or your side winning the Premiership, which would you choose?   Q.P.R. to win the Premiership.

Would you ground share with your rivals?   We shared with Fulham and they never put it on us to have a meet.

PART NINE

BURNLEY

RIVALS

BLACKBURN ROVERS

Name: **Pot**

Club: **Burnley**

We Mobbed Up At! I met Pot outside a pub near to Turfmoor and from there we moved onto the Burnleywood Club which is where, in 2001, some of the worst race riots ever seen in this country took place. Lots of houses have been either knocked down or boarded up and loads of people shipped out.

History/Honours? F.A. Cups, League Cups, promotions, the old First Division, Sherpa Van Final, we've won the lot. We were founded in 1882 and have had many famous and international players wear the claret and blue.

Background? Born and bred in Burnleywood, my whole family followed the football team except my brother who were a Derby fan. I left school with seven C.S.E.s and I'm now 38 years old. My first job was a shoe maker but I've done various jobs including working at Luton Airport, building sites, roofing, and caring for my dad who 'as M.S. and has just gone into a home, plus I've done various times in prison. It's hard to find work once you've been in jail.

Biggest rivals?   Blackburn Rovers because they bought the Premiership title. They've got no fans and what they have got are scum.

First game you ever went to?   I went with me mate's dad when I were about six and I remember us against Man. United, Man. City and Leeds.

Memories of first game against rivals?   In 1974 me and me mate and his dad went on the football special. Beside the ground was a fairground, and when we got there I remember the Blackburn fans coming out from the fair and bombarding us with bricks. Afterwards there were Burnley fans everywhere and we chased the scum everywhere. The police on horses couldn't contain the trouble. We had 'em everyway.

Finest team performance against them?   I don't bother about football. I don't really watch football, I'd much rather get beat because then all our lot are up for a row. People are happy when ya win. I'd rather get beat because then everyone's revved up for a battle.

Best goal?   No, I can't recall one. I'd rather watch the crowd as I don't give a flying fuck for football.

Worst defeat?   We lost 5-1 in a Youth Cup game and eight hundred of us went over there but Blackburn never turned out like they said they were going to. We all left at half time and went off and got pissed.

Biggest crowd? Probably about twenty eight thousand down at our place.

Best row, inside or outside the ground? '83, we ripped the roof off the stands. Two hundred of our lot got off the train at Acky and a hundred stayed on and got off at Blackburn. We chased the police off and out the ground and took over Nutall Street stand, which is the home end. It went mad and Norman Jones, one of our main boys, calmed the crowd down so that the game could carry on. It were just mental, fans climbed onto the roof and chucked lumps of slate and asbestos down onto the pitch. I've never seen anything like it. Celtic were another game. Ten thousand Jocks came down in '78 and took over every part of the ground except the Longside, which we defended and held for the whole of the game. They tried everything to budge us, including ripping up the metal fencing and using it as spears. That were one mental game as well.

Have you ever been injured at a game, or nicked? I got slashed above the eye at a game at Halifax who class us as one of their main rivals due to the fact that we're in Lancashire right on the Yorkshire border. I went into a boozer with a mate and a couple of other Burnley boys, sat down with a pint, and were just rolling a joint, when I heard someone say, "fuck off ya Yorkshire puddings". "Fuck off ya Lancashire cunts" came back the reply, and that was it. A boot came around the corner and kicked me in the face, glass was going everywhere, and knives were flashed as I was slashed above the eye. There was blood pissing out everywhere as I sought revenge running from pub to pub looking for the culprits. That was until I was grabbed by the Old Bill and taken off in an ambulance. Carlisle was another place where I came unstuck. I was sixteen and had me teeth knocked out by a mob of Carlisle. We'd run them everywhere and the police split our lot up. Three of us went off to find a drink and twenty Carlisle appeared. They chased us, I was tripped up and had me face kicked in. I lost me teeth but still got up and were rucking when the Old Bill turned up. I was in a hell of a state but still went to the ground. We were battling all day with them and I tell ya, Carlisle aint no dickhead place to go to. It's just a game, I love to fight and that's it.

What are your local Old Bill like?   Nobheads. Since that young Forest lad were killed the police here are on ya case all the time. The government 'as funded the police up here big time and now they teach other police forces up and down the country how to deal with football hooliganism. Also against Sheffield Wednesday, an old lady was hit by an ashtray and sadly died, and what with the race riots, which took sixty-eight of us off the streets, the police now run the show.

Name a player from their team you dislike or hate   Colin Hendrey.

Your favourite all time player?   Trever Steven. He was so skilful what with Kevin Reeves and Billy Hamilton we beat Tottenham 4-1.

Have any of their managers, past or present, really got up your nose?   All their past managers, they just bought the title and then they just fell apart. They just come for the money and without Jack Walker's money they'd still be down with us.

The worst song or chant their fans sing?   "Till We Play Burnley Bastards". I can't wait 'till we play 'em, the wankers. They just don't want to meet us; it's just a song.

Your favourite song or chant about them?   I aint got one, but our crowd sing "We Hate Bastards" and we've sung that for years. We never played them for seventeen years but the crowds still sang songs about the bastards. They have no history and no lads.

What's the furthest you've travelled to watch your team?
Plymouth, they always give us a good battle down there and I've
seen them turn up here, first game of the season, and do us. I
take me hat off to them, a good set of lads.

**Are you a season ticket holder and do you think your Club
could do more for its fans?** Me mum started working on turn-
stiles when I were about ten so she'd slip me in for nothing, and
I think the Club should invest in some decent players.

Have you ever worn a replica shirt? No, I've never worn a shirt
at a game but I've worn one on holiday. It's good to show off ya
Club colours on your holidays. What's wrong with that?

Have you ever cried at a game? No, never cried openly. I was
emotional when we had to beat Orient to stay in the football
league a few years back. The gate was eighteen thousand and we
all went on the pitch at the end. The police couldn't hold us back
when we won.

Do you take your children to football? Yes I have when I was
working down at Luton. I took them to watch Luton and they've
been with me to watch Burnley down at Barnsley. We went with
a coach load of hooligans and they loved it.

What would you do if a family member married a Rival? It
wouldn't happen.

Do you look out for any other teams' results? Yea, Wolves. I
was banged up with a Wolves' lad out in Sweden in '92 and we
just bonded and stayed friends since. I know our lot don't like
Wolves because our lot are pals with Tranmere's crew and
Tranmere have a thing going with Wolves. I've been with Wolves
at an England game and Tranmere and Burnley joined up

against Wolves and I stood with me Wolves mates which split the Burnley mob, half sided with me and half stayed with Tranmere.

Are there any other teams you dislike?   Carlisle, Stockport, Preston, Blackpool, Blackburn. I hate every team we've ever played. They know who I am so they can have it. I just go somewhere to do a job. For me I love the violence, simple as that. You hear people are waiting for ya and it's like putting a threat on ya doorstep, so you go just to do the job, it's that simple. It's a drink, a laugh, a punch up, and football comes second.

If there's one player in the world, past or present, that you could sign, who would it be?   Maradona. He's good with his feet and his hands.

If you had the choice of the National team winning the World Cup or your side winning the Premiership, which would you choose?   England to win the World Cup. I want to see us win it before I die. I'm English and proud of it.

Would you ground share with your rivals?   I'd love to share with them! No, not really, I wouldn't share a pub with them.

Name: **Johnie**

Club: **Blackburn Rovers**

We Mobbed Up At! Johnie, after some persuasion, ventured into hostile territory and met up with me at the Burnleywood Club. As we sat chatting he looked around and laughed. "Look at 'em" he said, "they're fucking dingles". There's definitely no love lost between these two Clubs.

History/Honours? '87 The Full Members' Cup against Charlton. 1995 the Premiership title. We've won more than fucking Burnley. They won the Sherpa Van Cup and got a new Sherpa van, big fucking deal.

Background? Born in Blackburn 35 years ago. I left school with four 'O' levels and have always been interested in football, playing it and watching it. I remember the Ronnie Clayton days.

Biggest rivals? Burnley.

First game you ever went to? I went with me mum to Bobby Moore's testimonial game when I was about seven at Ewood Park.

Memories of first game against rivals? Them smashing the roof in and wrecking the ground. One of their lads got onto the pitch and helped restore order and they kept all our lot in at the end of the game to stop us getting at them. We had the right fucking hump.

Finest team performance against them? I've missed both of our finest performances against them because I was banged up. We hadn't played them for seventeen years and we beat them twice in that season. When we beat them at Burnley, Andy Payton was substituted and as he came off he was mouthing off to the Blackburn fans. My mate that were there said he was covered in spit.

Best goal? Simon Garner in the Manx Cup. It was a local Cup competition with the finals on the Isle of Man and Preston, Bolton, and Burnley all used to take part. Also, when he left he went to play for Wycombe Wanderers and when he scored against Burnley at Turfmoor he lifted his shirt up and underneath he had on a Rovers' shirt. They went fucking mad. He was a top man and when we won the Premiership he stopped on the steps of the town hall with thousands of fans and sang "Chim Chimney, Chim Chimney, Chim Chim Charoo, We Hate Those Bastards in Claret and Blue". He used to come into my mate's shop for a chat and a fag; he's a top, top fella. He still slags off Burnley to this day.

Worst defeat? The time when they ripped the roof down. They've won a few times but normally we beat them so we haven't lost that many times to them.

Biggest crowd?   About twenty eight thousand at our place.

Best row, inside or outside the ground?   We never really get to fight, there's that many police. We did meet them at Rishton Station and had a row with them and turned them over, but we don't take it as serious as the Burnley mob. We're more interested in earning a few bob, wearing nice clobber, driving nice cars, and enjoying our football. They're just dingles. You know they just get bladdered and it's just out and out thuggery with them. In Burnley every other fucking house is boarded up, it's the way of life for them, cheap booze and a puff.

Have you ever been injured at a game, or nicked?   Yea, fighting with Bolton and I've been nicked a few times.

What are your local Old Bill like?   Horrible, they don't like football fans. I have 'em come into my yard for parts and I charge them double, as ya do.

Name a player from their team you dislike or hate Me, I don't dislike anyone.

Your favourite all time player? Simon Garner, a local boy done good, and I'd give David Speedie a mention; he didn't give a fuck for anyone.

Have any of their managers, past or present, really got up your nose? Not really, but some of our crowd have sung songs about John Bond and also about Stan Ternant. I just laugh at them all and take the piss out of 'em.

The worst song or chant their fans sing? When they sing about "Hating those Bastards in Blue and White". They've got some front; they just get cocky.

Your favourite song or chant about them?   Simon Garner's favourite "Chim Chimney We Hate Those Bastards in Claret and Blue", etc. etc.

What's the furthest you've travelled to watch your team?   I went out to Lyon in France for a E.U.F.A. Cup game.

Are you a season ticket holder, and do you think your Club could do more for its fans?   Not any more and yes, the Club could do more by reducing admission prices for the kids and O.A.P.s. I took me missus to see us against Celtic and it cost me £70, which is outrageous just to watch football.

Have you ever worn a replica shirt?   No, never.

Have you ever cried at a game?   When I got kicked to fuck against Middlesborough and I cried when we beat Leicester in the play-offs.

Do you take your children to football?   They're too young at the moment but my daughter wears the Blackburn kit.

What would you do if a family member married a Rival?   It wouldn't bother me; I wouldn't care.

Do you look out for any other teams' results?   Yes, Celtic. Me uncle was once assistant manager up there; he was Jock Stein's right-hand man.

Are there any other teams you dislike?   Bolton. We used to get on well with the Bolton fans, that were until we went with some Bolton lads to watch them play Burnley at Turfmoor. Anyway, the Burnley fans on the Longside clocked us lot down the front and started singing and chanting to the Bolton fans that we were Blackburn bastards and that they should get into us. They were pointing and shouting at us and were going fucking mental. The fifteen or so of us were suddenly swept further down the ter- races as the Bolton hordes swept down and steamed into us. A few Bolton lads that knew us broke it up and stood with us, but we'd well and truly been grassed up by the Burnley bastards.

If there's one player in the world, past or present, that you could sign, who would it be? Alan Shearer in his prime.

If you had the choice of the National team winning the World Cup or your side winning the Premiership, which would you choose? Blackburn winning the Premiership. I love England but I think we've gone backwards under Eriksson.

Would you ground share with your rivals? Would I fuck? You wouldn't do that would ya? They're fucking dingles. Some Blackburn fans are ugly fuckers but this Burnley mob takes the fucking biscuit. We used to come down here in the 80s dressed in all the latest Burberry and Boss and Armani gear, and these tramps used to think we were foreigners.

PART TEN

GLASGOW RANGERS

RI V ALS

CELTIC

Name: **Jimmy The Jock**

Club: **Glasgow Rangers**

We Mobbed Up At! In South Chelsea, well Battersea really, but the locals like to call it South Chelsea just to be on the posh side! We drank in a quiet little pub in the village, well it was peaceful until Jim walked in and the air turned as blue as his Rangers' shirt. Here, in his own words, is Jimmy's account of following the "Gers".

History/Honours? 50 Scottish League titles, 31 times Scottish F.A. Cup winners. The Scottish League Cup, 23 times and E.U.F.A. Cup once, and runners up twice.

Background? I was born 15 miles West of Glasgow in Greenock. I'm 52 and have 15 brothers and sisters. I left school with no qualifications and went straight onto a building site as a tea boy. All my family are Rangers fans.

Biggest rivals?   Celtic of course. It's all to do with religion; it's as simple as that.

First game you ever went to?   A Greenock – Morton game was the first match I ever went to. I bunked in with my mates.

Memories of first game against rivals?   I was about 15 when we played them at Ibrox and there was about 60,000 people there.

Finest team performance against them?   The semi final of the Scottish F.A. Cup in 1999 when Ali McCoist and Albertz scored. That was some performance, especially the German's thirty-yard free kick.

Best goal?   Albertz's free kick or a Laudrup header against Celtic.

Worst defeat?   Martin O'Neil's first game in charge in an old Firm game, and we lost 6-2.

Biggest crowd?   Probably about 80,000 at Park Head, when it was all standing.

Best row, inside or outside the ground   There's a lot of trouble between the two teams but the last one I was involved in was a few years back, when my Son was about twelve. We were on a bus going through Glasgow, on our way to the match, and a lot of Celtic supporters got on and came upstairs where we were sitting. They saw our colours and started kneeling down and blessing themselves and all that crap. We told them to leave it out and to behave, but they didn't listen, carried on and that was it. It kicked off big time, bodies were going everywhere as the bus rocked to the rhythm of the battle. We pulled up outside Park Head and their lot jumped off and with loads more joining in, began to attack the bus with bricks and bottles. We were lucky to get away that day I can tell you.

Have you ever been injured at a game, or nicked?   Yeah at a Celtic v Rangers game at Park Head. It was about eighteen years ago and Celtic won 3-1. Brian McClair took two dives to win two penalties, Terry Butcher scored an own goal, and a fan jumped on the pitch to get at Mclair and was jumped on by the police. Now with all this going on right in front of me I couldn't see the game so I asked a copper if he could get out of the road so that I could see the game. He leant over the wall, grabbed me and said "I'll give you, throwing coins at a policeman", and he dragged me out. I was taken on a police bus to London Road Police Station, photographed, and asked if I was a left footer or a right footer. "Right footer" I replied, meaning that I was a Rangers' fan. "Right, in there", and I was pushed into a cell with other fans that had been arrested. When we were in there a group of blokes were accusing another prisoner of being a Celtic fan and insults led to punches as the bloke took a kicking, still denying he was a left footer. He was carried from the cell on a stretcher and as he left, the police searched him again and pulled out a blue and white Rangers' scarf, which had been tucked down his trousers. The lengths people go to to get out of police custody! After sixteen hours I was released because my young Son was waiting outside for me on his own. I later pleaded guilty by post for something I'd nay done. If I'd have gone "not guilty" I'd have to have taken time off work and maybe it would have taken maybe a couple of court appearances, and even then the court would have believed the lying fucking coppers' tale of events. If I ever saw that lying fucking scumbag I'd spit in his eye.

What are your local Old Bill like?   Fucking arse-holes.

Name a player from their team you dislike or hate.   Neil Lennon. I can't stand the Irish cunt.

Your favourite all time player?   Gazza, he's the man that played the flute. He's a folk hero in some parts of Glasgow.

Have any of their managers, past or present, really got up your nose? Martin O'Neil. He jumps up and down on the touchline like a Jack in the box when Celtic scores a goal. He's like a big kid.

The worst song or chant their fans sing? Any fucking I.R.A. song. What's that got to do with football in Scotland?

Your favourite song or chant about them? There are two. The song about "The Sash my Father Wore" and "Who shagged all the boys?". They get the right hump about them two.

What's the furthest you've travelled to watch your team? Copenhagen in a European tie.

Are you a season ticket holder, and do you think your Club could do more for its fans? No, never had a season ticket but some of my family are. Maybe the Ibrox' stewards could be told to leave off a bit when the boys are singing songs at the Celtic fans, and the stewards can sometimes be a bit too quick to chuck people out for singing certain songs at them.

Have you ever worn a replica shirt? Yes, I do wear a shirt at football and sometimes to work, but the best one is if Rangers beat Celtic. My nephews will wear their England shirts and tracksuits out in the pubs of Glasgow.

Have you ever cried at a game? I wouldna' say cry, but when Hearts beat us in the Cup Final, which was Walter Smith's last game in charge, that was the worst feeling in the world and I did feel like crying.

Do you take your children to football? Yes, but a few years back me and the boy couldn't get tickets for an auld Firm game and a well known London ticket tout, as a last resort, promised me two, but what he forgot to mention was that they were in the Celtic end. Well to cut a long story short, we were spat on and terrorised for the whole game. That nearly put me off taking the kids to football.

What would you do if a family member married a Rival? Unless I wanted to have a fight then I would stay away from the wedding. You know there's going to be trouble.

Do you look out for any other teams' results?   Chelsea. I'm a big Chelsea fan and I had a season ticket for eight years when the boy was young. I've held one now for the past five years. I also watch out for Greenock Morton.

Are there any other teams you dislike?   Man. United and Arsenal. I can't stand them and since Ferguson took over at Man. United I can't stand them. He's a Blue Nose with a blue nose, if you get my drift!

If there's one player in the world, past or present, that you could sign, who would it be?   That would be Gazza or Davie Cooper. The pair of them were brilliant.

If you had the choice of the National team winning the World Cup or your side winning the Premiership, which would you choose?   That's easy, Rangers winning the Premiership, every time.

Would you ground share with your rivals?   No way, I wouldn't give Celtic a penny.

Name: **Ricky**

Club: **Celtic**

We Mobbed Up At! We met in Battersea, South London, in a friendly little pub just around the corner from the Arts Centre. We had a few beers and Ricky told me about his football days and his life in Glasgow.

History/Honours? Celtic Football Club was founded in 1888 by a Catholic priest. In 1967 we won the European Cup, beating Inter Milan, and have won every domestic honour a multitude of times. Far too many in fact to mention.

Background? I'm 39 years old and come from Castlemilk, which is about a mile from Hampden. I left school with no qualifications and my first job was in the old Singers' place, doing a decorators' course. Painting and decorating is what I still do now and I've lived in London for 22 years.

Biggest rivals?   Rangers. They're Protestant and Celtic are Catholic; it's the way I've been brought up.

First game you ever went to?   I can't remember which teams would have been playing but I can remember sitting on my dad's shoulders watching the game. Another memory that's stayed with me was when I was about 9 or 10 and I watched my dad pulling half a bottle of wine from his coat pocket and drinking it whilst watching the game. I was watching him more that I was watching the football!

Memories of first game against rivals?   My first memory was trying to bunk in and some fucker pulling me back by the scarf I had wrapped around my neck. As I tried to jump over the turnstile I was nearly strangled. I must have been about twelve then and he wouldn't let go, the blue nosed bastard.

Finest team performance against them?   The 6-2 recent one was a good one, but the one that sticks in my mind was when Terry Butcher and Graham Roberts were playing for Rangers and Roberts had to go in goal, and we won 3-2.

Best goal?   The Henrick Larrson goal when he ran with the ball, nutmegged one of them, and chipped it into the net. He was just taking the piss and it was just brilliant to watch.
Worst defeat?   There's been a few but probably the recent 4-2 defeat, that hurt.

Biggest crowd?   Around about 60,000 with the old terrace, which we called the Jungle, packed to the rafters. The atmosphere was great and as people couldn't move, men had to piss in empty beer cans and throw them down the front.

Best row, inside or outside the ground?   I've been chased a few times by Rangers' fans, and a few years ago we left the ground and were walking up the London Road when a mob came running towards us. I could hear cockney accents so I knew there were Chelsea fans in with the Rangers' boys; there were hundreds of them. "Stand, stand, hang about" said a few of our boys, trying to make a stand. People were running everywhere to get away, back towards the ground, into shops and jumping on buses, as we did. As we drove along the road I looked back and could see them attacking people at bus stops. Ever since then I've fucking hated Chelsea.

Have you ever been injured at a game, or nicked? No, never been nicked or injured. Just out of breath from running from them Chelsea bastards.

What are your local Old Bill like? All blue nosed bastards.

Name a player from their team you dislike or hate. Fucking hell, where do you want me to start? Ian Ferguson, he was a right dirty fucker. Once he was chasing the ball and it went off the pitch and his momentum took him into the fence, and he gave the Celtic fans packed behind it a right filthy look. The fans went mad, spitting and gobbing on him and giving him the wanker's sign. Also, Gascoigne when he was at Rangers. I hated him, he was a quality player but a bit of a nutcase, but still if I met him I'd have no problem shaking his hand.

Your favourite all time player? Kenny Dalglish, pure class.

Have any of their managers, past or present, really got up your nose? Souness, because as a player he was one dirty bastard.

The worst song or chant their fans sing? That fucking stupid "Sash" song or "The Blood of the Finnean Bastards" or "Surrender or You'll Die". What do they want us to do, say "O.K." and stick our hands up? Fucking idiots.

Your favourite song or chant about them   "King Billy Had an Army of a Thousand Men. They all Got Shot Bang Bang".

What's the furthest you've travelled to watch your team?   Not that far, probably Aberdeen. When I was a kid I nicked the money from my paper round to pay to go up to Aberdeen to watch Celtic.

Are you a season ticket holder, and do you think your Club could do more for its fans?   No I've never had a season ticket, but they should sign better players and splash the cash and maybe reduce ticket prices. There's still people in Glasgow with nothing who'd love to go to watch Celtic play.

Have you ever worn a replica shirt?   Yes I have but not as a kid because I couldn't afford one. As a rule I don't, the green and white is a bit loud.

Have you ever cried at a game?   No, but I've prayed a few times.

Do you take your children to football?   My kids do go. Celtic and Rangers games are not as bad as they used to be.

What would you do if a family member married a Rival?   No problem, I've been living with a Blue Nose for the last twelve years.

Do you look out for any other teams' results?   Liverpool. A lot of the Scousers are Catholics.

Are there any other teams you dislike?   Chelsea because of their fans having this thing with Rangers.

If there's one player in the world, past or present, that you

could sign, who would it be?   Maradona in his prime, he was the greatest.

If you had the choice of the National team winning the World Cup or your side winning the Premiership, which would you choose?   Scotland to win the World Cup, but I'd take Celtic to win the Champions' League. Us winning the Scottish League is getting boring, we've won it so many times.

Would you ground share with your rivals   Fuck me, no one would share with them bitter animals, they're so bitter it's unbelievable.

PART ELEVEN

PORTSMOUTH

RI V ALS

SOUTHHAMPTON

Name: **Rob Silvester**

Club: **Portsmouth**

We Mobbed Up At! The Shepherds Crook Pub, a stone's throw from Fratton Park. I've known Rob for a few years now and while Pompey are entertaining Everton, we're out in the beer garden sinking a few beers and talking about the 657 book which has just come out in paperback. Plug over! We get down to talking football and more importantly, the Scummers.

History/Honours? We held the F.A. Cup for six years because of the Second World War. We won the old First Division Championship twice and should have won it a third time but lost out by as couple of points.

Background? I was born in Finchley, North London. My mum's family moved to America and my Nan wouldn't fly, she would only sail. My mum and dad got divorced and we ended up

living down here. I'm now a best selling author, married and live
locally.

Biggest rivals?   Southampton.

First game you ever went to?   When I was six I went to watch
Spurs play at White Hart Lane. My dad was in the flying squad
(The Sweeney) and we'd go by car and park in the magistrates'
court just up the road from the ground. As we drove in, the man
on the gate would tip his hat and give a salute. The first Pompey
game I ever went to was Swansea at home in the Cup. I went
with a local youth club and the famous story was how the bloke
with the swan on a stick got it smashed over his head. I was
about ten.

Memories of first game against rivals?   When Mick Channon
scored in the last minute. It was 1976, the year they won the F.A.
Cup. After the game ended the Fratton end emptied and went
around to the Milton Road end where they were. Some got in
and just let them have it and it was the first time I'd seen pure
football violence. I heard the sound of running and shouting
from behind me and three Pompey geezers kicked the fuck out
of a Scummer who they'd chased and caught. I've heard many
reasons why there's so much hatred between the two clubs or
even between the two cities. One reason is that their dockers
came down to the Portsmouth docks and crossed the picket line
and helped break a strike, which I believe was in the late 50s,
early 60s. Geographically, Tichfield, the last Portsmouth post-
code area before Southampton, is only eight miles from them
and the people of Tichfield still burn an effigy of the Earl of
Southampton at their yearly carnival. It's said that he tried to cut
the river off at Tichfield.

Finest team performance against them?   When we beat them 2-
0 at the Dell. It was around Christmas time in the old first divi-

sion and we got there early and wandered around unopposed. They're renowned for not turning up.

Best Goal? Terry Connor's goal which put us 2-0 up.

Worst defeat? Losing 1-0 to them in the Cup. It was another last minute goal that beat us. We had a massive mob out that day but another no show from them.

Biggest crowd? Probably twenty odd thousand at the Dell and about thirty odd at Fratton Park.

Best row, inside or outside the ground? It would be us just looking for them. We have to hunt them and we've even been there on a Friday night looking for them. They've got some individual game geezers but they can't seem to put a mob together for any game. No team should get done at home but they do every other week.

Have you ever been injured at a game, or nicked? I was nicked at the Alan Knight Testimonial game over there. They never showed so we got fighting with the Old Bill and I got a hundred hours community service. Six of us were coming back from a game at Cardiff and got off the train at Southampton and they'd been playing Tottenham at home that day. We walked into their main pub, which was packed, and were recognised almost straight away and were bombarded with glasses and bottles. They wouldn't come into us and fight; they just threw gear at us. The whole pub turned on us and I got eighteen stitches in my head. Another of our boys got seventy stitches in his face and out of the six of us, five got severely injured.

What are your local Old Bill like? Because Pompey is an island there's no major crime so the police have nothing to do but chase football mobs or our main faces about. They love a video camera and you can't go anywhere without having one shoved in your face.

Name a player from their team you dislike or hate.   Francis Benali because he portrays what a Scummer looks like, moustache, dark skinned, mixed race.

Your favourite all time player?   Robert Propseneki, a Croatian, and the best player I've ever seen at Fratton Park.

Have any of their managers, past or present, really got up your nose?
Alan Ball because he once said that Southampton were the biggest club on the south coast.

The worst song or chant their fans sing?   "When the Saints Go Marchin' In". That's like a kids' Sunday school song, it's so fucking boring.

Your favourite song or chant about them?   Any player that's ever played for Southampton and turns out against Pompey gets untold abuse. Look at Wayne Bridge. When he plays for Chelsea against us he get the "Scummer Scummer" chant. We don't let him or any of the other misfits forget that we hate Southampton.

What's the furthest you've travelled to watch your team?
Carlisle. We used to go everywhere away in me mate's yellow, Mark Three Cortina.

Are you a season ticket holder, and do you think your Club could do more for its fans?   No never had a season ticket. Stop all the bullshit and build a new ground. The club should match the fans' ambitions. They've been promising a new stadium for the last twenty years.

Have you ever worn a replica shirt? No, never to a game, but I've worn one playing football and down the pub.

Have you ever cried at a game? No, never.

Do you take your children to football? Yes I've taken my eldest son and he met all the players in the players' lounge after the game.

What would you do if a family member married a Rival? Turn her around and make her see sense and convert her.

Do you look out for any other teams' results? Glasgow Rangers for obvious reasons.

Are there any other teams you dislike? Celtic for obvious reasons.

If there's one player in the world, past or present, that you could sign, who would it be? Roy Carroll, the Man. United keeper and I hear he's a good flute player, or Rio Ferdinand, a world-class defender who's got it all.

If you had the choice of the National team winning the World Cup or your side winning the Premiership, which would you choose? Portsmouth for the Premiership, I'm British not just English.

Would you ground share with your rivals? I can't see it happening. They wouldn't share Fratton Park with us and the ground would be empty until one minute to three when they'd start sneaking in. They're below Wimbledon, Watford and Wycombe Wanderers in the Hoolie stakes. Theirs is one hooligan book that won't come out, and if they did release something it would only be a pamphlet.

Name: **Ray**

Club: **Southampton**

We Mobbed Up At! We met at the Imperial pub, which is known as the Lemon, in Crawley, Sussex. I met Ray through my mate Fordy. When we sat down Ray told me he became a Southampton fan after they'd beaten his then team, Man. Utd. in the 1976 Cup final. He'd worked out that it was easier to see the Saints play than it was getting up to Manchester but he thinks now that it was a mistake and he should have stuck with them.

History/Honours? 1976 F.A. Cup winners, we finished 2nd in the league to Liverpool in '79. We once had eleven ex England captains in the team.

Background? Born in Crawley and lived here all my life. I'm 42 years old, and left school with a G.S.E. in maths. My dad owned a transport company, which I joined when I left school and I now run my own transport company.

Biggest rivals? Portsmouth.

First game you ever went to? Palace v Arsenal. Willie Young was playing for Arsenal and it was 2-1 to the Gunners. I went with "Red Mick", a big Arsenal fan.

Memories of first game against rivals? It would have been at the Dell but we hadn't really played them that much due to them languishing in the lower leagues.

Finest team performance against them? Last season when we beat them 3-1 at St. Mary's. They were gutted, still fuck 'em.

Best goal? I reckon James Beattie's goal in the same 3-1 win. Beattie scored a typical James Beattie goal with his head.

Worst defeat? The return fixture at Fratton Park. It was like they'd won the F.A. Cup, the League and the Champions' League all rolled into one. They don't get a lot of success and it painfully shows.

Biggest crowd? I would think forty odd thousand when it was terracing at their place and just under thirty thousand at St. Mary's.

Best row, inside or outside the ground? I was never directly involved in any trouble. I would drive to the game, go straight in and drive off straight after the game finished. Most Saints fans aint looking for trouble and are just there for the football, where-as Pompey are hell-bent on violence. We love our football, clothes, music, women, and cars. They love the booze and the punch ups. We're a totally different type of crowd to them. They hate the good people of Southampton because of a dock strike that happened years ago. They said we nicked their jobs which may be so, but I've also heard it said that some of them were lazy bastards that didn't want to work anyway. They have a hardcore hooligan element that carries that bad feeling on, but last season I heard that their main boys came unstuck at St. Mary's last time we played. What's the old saying? "You can only kick a dog so many times before it turns around and bites you." We go purely for the football, not for the trouble. Have a look around St. Mary's on a home game; it's a different class of people down our place.

Have you ever been injured at a game, or nicked?   No, never been nicked or injured watching Southampton but I've copped a few punches on the nose from rival fans watching our local side, Crawley.

What are your local Old Bill like?   From what I've seen they're very fair. When we play Portsmouth the police presence is huge and then they probably approach the game differently and act accordingly.

Name a player from their team you dislike or hate.   Eyal Berkovic, he's an ex-Saint who has done the rounds at Man. City, West Ham and now Portsmouth. How can he play for them?

Your favourite all time player?   Le God, Matt Le Tissier. When Hoddle was manager at Chelsea he was going to build a side around him and apparently Chelsea were willing to pay £10 million for him. He was sheer class, a one off.

Have any of their managers, past or present, really got up your nose?   Alan Ball. We didn't want an old Portsmouth manager in charge of us.

The worst song or chant their fans sing? "Scummers, Scummers", that's old hat now. I just want to watch the football, not listen to them cunts.

Your favourite song or chant about them? The song about "We Nicked all Your Jobs" and "There's Only One Team in Hampshire".

What's the furthest you've travelled to watch your team? I don't do away games. I like my own space and don't like being herded about and packed in with hordes of bodies like sardines.

Are you a season ticket holder, and do you think your Club could do more for its fans? No, not really. We've got a fantastic stadium but we could do with installing a world-class manager and then we could get a better class of player in. I'd even take Hoddle back as we played good football under him. He done well for us and must have a future in football somewhere.

Have you ever worn a replica shirt? Yes I do wear one but they're like rocking horse shit. You can't find one in the sports shops unless you go to the club shop. In my locals sports shops you can find Real Madrid, Barcelona, and Man. Utd. shirts but you won't find a Saints shirt anywhere.

Have you ever cried at a game? Not at Southampton but I shed tears of joy when Man. Utd. beat Munich in the European Cup Final. It was the fighting spirit right up until the last minute. I've still got a soft spot for the Reds and still remember the stories my old granddad used to tell me about the old United players.

Do you take your children to football? They're only seven and eight but when they're older they'll be going. They've been guided now towards being Saints fans.

What would you do if a family member married a Rival? We'd have a right laugh, plenty of banter, a right piss take. Life and football aint about being too serious.

Do you look out for any other teams' results? Man. United, obviously. Chelsea because they play good football and I watch Real Madrid twice a week on T.V. because I can.

Are there any other teams you dislike? Man. City. Nothing to do with the United connection, I just think the collection of so-called stars they've got there are just crap. They're appalling and they're just there for the money. And Arsenal because they never lose a game.

If there's one player in the world, past or present, that you could sign, who would it be? David Beckham. I love him, he's great, a fantastic player, and he's still got it.

If you had the choice of the National team winning the World Cup or your side winning the Premiership, which would you choose? England winning the World Cup. It would bring people together; everyone would come out with the flags and the cars all decorated. It would be great for the whole country. We're living on a winning memory from over thirty years ago and with the players we've got we should be able to win it. The rest of the world hates us.

Would you ground share with your rivals? No, ground sharing don't work. Inter Milan share with A.C. Milan but it wouldn't work between us and Pompey.

PART TWELVE

SHEFFIELD WEDNESDAY

 RI V ALS

SHEFFIELD UNITED

Name: **Sesh**

Club: **Sheffield Wednesday**

We Mobbed Up At! The Hilton Hotel. I drove up to Sheffield to see Sesh in his home City. I've met Sesh before, he was with a Wednesday mate of his and four Chelsea faces when they were caught in the underground by a very embarrassed and irate mob of 200 Sheffield United lads who, only half an hour earlier, had been battered to fuck by fifty Chelsea boys. The six of them held the doors of the tube as they came under attack by the United hordes. Sesh was knocked to the ground and after receiving a good kicking, had his trainers stolen from his feet. So there's the real story Mr. Cowans, so now who was telling the truth? Sesh also told me that he got to know, over the course of time, who was actually responsible for removing the said shoes and he has chased the culprit through the streets of Sheffield but, alas, has yet to get hold of him. He also added that his pride was dented, not by being put on his arse by a United fan, but by having to wear green flash Dunlop trainers as replacements for his stolen shoes.

History/Honours? F.A. Cup 1935, League Cup in 1991, a few promotions, and losing finals in various Cups.

Background? I was born and bred in Sheffield in Sheffield 6, Hillsborough. I left school with a few C.S.E.s in English, Maths and History. My first job was a warehouse man on a Y.T.S. Scheme. I'm now 37 and have a brother who's Wednesday through and through.

Biggest rivals? Sheffield United. I learnt from me dad to hate 'em.

First game you ever went to? It were against Swindon and I went with me dad and younger brother and that was about '77. We'd been before but that game sticks in my memory.

Memories of first game against rivals? Boxing Day '79 and we beat them 4-0. We had played them for ages and their then Manager, Harry Haslam, came out smiling. They were near the top of the league but we soon wiped that smug look off his face.

Finest team performance against them? Wembley, April 3rd '93. We beat them 2-1 in the semi-final of the F. A. Cup. That was a great team performance and Waddle and Bright got the goals.

Best Goal? Chris Waddle's free kick from 40 yards in that semi-final game.

Worst defeat? 3-1 at Hillsborough and Bobby Davidson scored twice in a midweek game, and last season when we lost 3-1 at the Lane and we fielded the worst Wednesday team I've ever seen in my life. There was no spirit in the side and they just didn't want to show any fight. In fact, they looked like they didn't want to play.

Biggest crowd?   When it were terrace at Hillsborough the crowd would be around forty odd thousand and we once had thirty-four thousand at a Zenith Data Cup match, which is still a record crowd attendance for that competition.

Best row, inside or outside the ground? Six of us were in Limit Nightclub in a back street when United's mob, about 200 strong, showed up and it went off and the six of us held it together in the doorway. We've never let them forget that one.

Have you ever been injured at a game, or nicked?   I've been bruised and had a few fat and cut lips, and I've been locked up a few times and oh yea, have I mentioned it, I once had me trainers nicked by some scumbag mob!

What are your local Old Bill like?   Disgusting, they're on everyone's case. I was locked up for ten hours for something I never done. They came to my work and took me away to the cells for an incident they said I'd been involved in at Derby the previous week. They produced their photographic evidence and were adamant it was me. The one thing that was wrong was that the photographs wasn't of me. They had the wrong person and had to let me go. Later that week they were forced to apologise. That really pissed me off at the time.

Name a player from their team you dislike or hate.   Carl Bradshaw. He played for us but when he went to United it was the comments he made about us and how, at every opportunity, he'd kiss the badge on his United shirt. When he were with us he was Wednesday till he died, then he joined them and he came out with he were United until he died.

Your favourite all time player? John Sheridan, a real class act.

Have any of their managers, past or present, really got up your nose? Neil Warnock, even if we're not playing them he comes out with something about Wednesday in interviews.

The worst song or chant their fans sing? "A Night Out in Sheffield with a Greasy Chip Butty". What the fuck that 'as to do with football I'll never know.

Your favourite song or chant about them? "Die Die Piggy Piggy Die Die".

What's the furthest you've travelled to watch your team? Kaiserslautern in Germany for a E.U.F.A. Cup match.

Are you a season ticket holder, and do you think your Club could do more for its fans? I'm not a season ticket holder but the Club should drop admission prices, especially with some of the football we watch. The Board seem more interested in making money than building a future for the Club.

Have you ever worn a replica shirt? I might have when I was a child but now I wouldn't be seen dead in one.

Have you ever cried at a game? I've had a tear in my eye when we've won promotion and got to Cup finals. It means a lot to me.

Do you take your children to football? I will when they're older.

What would you do if a family member married a Rival? I'd go to the wedding and take the piss.

Do you look out for any other teams' results? Yea, Chelsea and

Birmingham. I know the Chelsea boys quiet well and I've got mates from Birmingham.

Are there any other teams you dislike?   Leeds and Celtic. The Leeds lot still rave on about how good they were in the 60s and 70s but that's all in the past. They've got to realise they're just a shit team now.

If there's one player in the world, past or present, that you could sign, who would it be?   John Sheridan. He came over here the other week scouting for Oldham and the man on the gate gave him grief. My mate pointed out that the man he was having a go at was a former Wednesday "great". "Who's John Sheridan?" the gate man replied.

If you had the choice of the National team winning the World Cup or your side winning the Premiership, which would you choose?   Wednesday winning the Premiership. I'm English through and through and I've followed England in the European Championship and World Cups, but for me, Wednesday winning the title would be something else.

Would you ground share with your rivals?   Never. I couldn't imagine sitting in the same seat as a United fan the week after they've played. No, never, it wouldn't work.

Name: **Ducker**

Club: **Sheffield United**

We Mobbed Up At!   The Hilton in Sheffield, straight after Sesh had done his bit. After suffering in silence here's what he said about following United.

History/Honours?   Honours don't come easy to a United-ite, we've not won nowt for many a moon, or any kind of glory. A few promotions and the odd semi-final but no, nothing to speak of. Not very good for a side founded in 1889.

Background?   I've been a Blade since the day I were born. I'm 33 years of age and I grew up in Sheffield 6, which is a predominately "Wednesday" area. My dad were a Blade and I liked the underdog spirit associated with United, and United fans tend to come from Sheffield itself whereas a lot of Wednesdays' support comes from outside the City. Well, that's how I see it anyway.

We've tolerated one another for years but now it's got more personal amongst some people. I left school with three 'O' levels in English, Maths and Biology. My first job was in a factory and I've done various work schemes.

Biggest rivals? Sheffield Wednesday.

First game you ever went to? The first game I ever remember going to was with me dad and brother, but I can't recall who were playing.

Memories of first game against rivals? The 4-0 defeat on Boxing Day at Hillsborough. It were awful and it pissed down with rain, it was just a dreadful day.

Finest team performance against them? It's got to be winning 3-0 at Wednesday. It was about '93 and was a great day for us lot.

Best goal? Probably one of Bobby Davidson's goals in that 3-1 win. They were nothing special, but it was lovely to see Wednesday crumble.

Worst defeat? Losing at Wembley in the semi-final to them lot. We'd played well all season but that day we had a bad day at the office, we were dreadful.

Biggest crowd? Probably 49,000 on boxing Day, 1979.

Best row, inside or outside the ground? It would have been the early nineties at Bramhall Lane. It started off in London Road as everyone came out of the ground at the same time. Wednesday came out down the bottom and a shop window went in and United steamed down at them, it was chaos. The Old Bill didn't have a clue and it went on for hours. They blocked roads off but they couldn't stop it and they looked lost as to how to stop it.

Have you ever been injured at a game, or nicked? I got a good kicking at Derby one year. Before the game about ten of us had been in a boozer not far from the ground. We came out heading off towards the match, turned a corner, and bumped straight into about 40 of their lot. We got fucking battered and it put us lot out of action for a while.

What are your local Old Bill like? Awful, legalised thugs, storm troopers, that's all they are. In the 80s they were different. They'd catch ya doing something, give ya a kicking, and send ya on ya way. Now they'll do ya for nowt. What with all these banning orders, they've banned so many people it's scandalous. These storm troopers that come out on match days, they're just looking for trouble. A few months ago one of these storm troopers, dressed in his riot gear, told one of our lot that if our mob were up for it today, then bring it on. Where do you go from there? They stand there with full body armour, riot truncheons, shields, and sprays, faces covered. What's it coming to?

Name a player from their team you dislike or hate Terry Curran, he came and played at the Lane for us but I hated him with a passion. He could have scored a fifty yarder for us or a hat trick every game and I still would have hated him.

Your favourite all time player? A bit before my time really, but I'd say Tony Currie. The image of him sitting on the ball while the game was going on sticks in my mind. He was such a skilful player and that day he was just taking the piss.

Have any of their managers, past or present, really got up your nose? Jack Charlton, he was in charge in about '79 when they done us on that Boxing Day. I hate anything to do with that game.

The worst song or chant their fans sing? It's got to be that

"Hark now Hear the Wednesday Sing". I reckon they nicked that one off us. Anyway they sing it that much it just gets up my nose.

Your favourite song or chant about them?   It's got to be the "Greasy Chip Buttie" song. It's just a song about having a fag and a pint and just being a working class lad. It echoes around the ground and it just stirs feelings up inside me, it's a great song.

What's the furthest you've travelled to watch your team? Probably Wembley. I've never been out of the country but I've followed them all over the country and that's not bad for following a team that's never really won nowt.

Are you a season ticket holder, and do you think your Club could do more for its fans?   I've had a season ticket just the once, many many moons ago, and the one thing the Club could do is stop selling our best players. How many times have they let some of our best players go on transfer deadline day?

Have you ever worn a replica shirt?   I've worn an England shirt and a United shirt on holiday but never one to a game. I did as a kid but not nowadays.

Have you ever cried at a game?   When Wednesday beat us in that semi-final, I just thought, "what happened here"? and I had to fight hard to hold back the tears.

Do you take your children to football?   If I had kids I would take them, but pick and choose which games. I wouldn't take them somewhere where they'd be at risk.

What would you do if a family member married a Rival?   It wouldn't be an issue; outside the terraces real life shouldn't come into it. I've never born a grudge to anyone because of the team they support.

Do you look out for any other teams' results?   Glasgow Rangers.

Are there any other teams you dislike? Leeds United, they're scum, they think they're so superior. Dream on.

If there's one player in the world, past or present, that you could sign, who would it be? Wayne Rooney, I wouldn't mind him in our side.

If you had the choice of the National team winning the World Cup or your side winning the Premiership, which would you choose? Blades winning the Premiership without a shadow of a doubt. I love England to pieces, but at the end of the day it's Club first.

Would you ground share with your rivals? No never. We've got the oldest recognised stadium in the world. It might not be up to Wednesdays' standards but it is getting a modern feel to it. Imagine being a season ticket holder and giving it up for a local Derby. No, no way. Being evicted from your own seat, it just wouldn't be on.

PART THIRTEEN

CRYSTAL PALACE

RI**V**ALS

BRIGHTON

Name: **Matt**

Club: **Crystal Palace**

We Mobbed Up At! We met in the Duke of Cambridge Pub in Holmesdale Road, just a stone's throw from the ground.

History/Honours? None really to speak of, a few promotions and losers in F.A. Cup finals.

Background? Born in South Norwood, I'm 34 years old and have been following Palace seriously for 10 years. I left school and went roofing and now I'm a scaffolder.

Biggest rivals? Brighton, and it goes back years, I suppose to the Malcolm Alison days or when Alan Mullery managed both Clubs, or maybe even before that. I don't know, but we hate them. On the terraces you can just feel the hatred towards them.

First game you ever went to?   I used to go to Palace with me dad when I was about twelve. One game that stuck out was when we played Watford and Elton John was in the dug out.

Memories of first game against rivals?   My first memories was how many Old Bill were on the streets around Thornton Heath. There was helicopters, dogs, horses, the lot, and we beat Brighton 5-0.

Finest team performance against them?   The 5-0 win, without a doubt.

Best goal?   Anyone in the 5-0 win, they were all great for me.

Worst defeat?   I don't care to remember. I tend to forget the bad days against them.

Biggest crowd?   Brighton only holds seven thousand and the old Goldstone didn't hold many. I suppose it would be at our place, which now holds about twenty seven thousand.

Best row, inside or outside the ground?   We smash them ever time. There's more of us than them.

Have you ever been injured at a game, or nicked?   I got done against Westham outside me house. Three West Ham lumps set about me on the corner of my road and they were giving me a bit of a kicking. My twelve year old boy 'as seen what's going on and hit one with a lump of wood, as I was laying on the floor. I've heard one of them go "oh! you little cunt", but I would say he helped save me from serious injury.

What are your local Old Bill like?   They're all right; they're pretty fair.

Name a player from their team you dislike or hate   Bobby Zamora, he went to Tottenham so that makes him horrible, and he scores goals.

Your favourite all time player?   Ian Wright, a great goal scorer who I was sorry to see go to Arsenal. Mark Dennis, a great player for Palace and a good mate of mine.

Have any of their managers, past or present, really got up your nose?   Mark McGhee, he's ex Millwall.

The worst song or chant their fans sing? "We hate Palace" and "Seagulls, Seagulls".

Your favourite song or chant about them? "We Will Follow the Palace Over Land and Sea and Brighton, We Will Follow the Palace Onto Victory".

What's the furthest you've travelled to watch your team? Liverpool, and we lost 5-0, but I missed it when we played them in the Cup and beat them with ten men, 2-0.

Are you a season ticket holder, and do you think your Club could do more for its fans?   Yes, I've got a season ticket, but they should improve the facilities inside the ground. You can go 20 minutes, half an hour, to get a beer. It's a joke.

Have you ever worn a replica shirt?   Yea, even to away games.

Have you ever cried at a game?   No, never, but I might cry when we play Chelsea because I'll be sitting next to my brother and uncle and they're both Chelsea.

Do you take your children to football? Yes, sometimes, but of course I pick and choose the games we go to.

What would you do if a family member married a Rival?
Disown them, no question; it's as simple as that.

Do you look out for any other teams' results?   Brighton, West
Ham. I look out to make sure they're losing!

Are there any other teams you dislike?   Brighton, Millwall and
Charlton, they're South East London rivals.

**If there's one player in the world, past or present, that you
could sign, who would it be?**   It's hard, but probably Zidane;
he's quality and we could do with someone like him now.

**If you had the choice of the National team winning the World
Cup or your side winning the Premiership, which would you
choose?**   Palace winning the Premiership, it's Club before
Country for me.

Would you ground share with your rivals?   Never, no fucking
way, fuck that. All them gay boys would be waiting for us; you'd
have to watch your arse down there.

Name: **Brighton Ben**

Club: **Brighton and Hove Albion**

We Mobbed Up At! I was introduced to Ben by a good mate of mine, Fordy.

History/Honours? Founded in 1902, runners up in F.A. Cup 1983, drew 2-2 and lost 4-0 in the replay, and various promotions in the last few years.

Background? Born in Brighton, I'm 27 years old.

Biggest rivals? Crystal Palace.

First game you ever went to? It was Newcastle United at home in the F.A. Cup and was the year we reached the Cup Final. I was six years old and went with my dad and brother. We drew 1-1 at the Goldstone and won 1-0 up there with a Peter Ward goal.

Memories of first game against rivals?   We beat them 2-0 with goals from Danny Wilson and Dean Saunders and my dad and brother watched it from the East Stand. Even at 10 years of age I could sense the hostility between the two sides.

Finest team performance against them?   I think I'd have to go back 17 years to that 2-0 win. The last time we played them at the Withdean we slaughtered them. We hit the bar and hit the post, we done everything except score, and it ended up 0-0.

Best goal?   Any goal we score against them is a good goal. If we scored a penalty against them I'd class that as a good goal.

Worst defeat?   Two years ago we lost 5-0. We hadn't played them for thirteen years. We were 2-0 down after five minutes when they went three up. The 7,500 Brighton fans there tried to leave but the police held us in half an hour after the game. When the fifth goal went in the Brighton fans were singing "We're Going to Win 6-5"!

Biggest crowd?   Probably thirty odd thousand at the Goldstone and maybe a bit more at Palace.

Best row, inside or outside the ground?   There's always trouble between the two teams and it goes back to the 70s. They're probably the nearest team to us geographically and there's real hatred between them and us. You always hear stories about where it's gone off and where the two mobs have met.

Have you ever been injured at a game, or nicked?   No, never been injured and never been nicked.

What are your local Old Bill like?   Two Bob. I was standing behind the goal in the North Stand at the Goldstone when an opponent's goalkeeper went to take a goal kick. The packed crowd shouted "whoa" as he started his run up and shouted "you're shit" as he kicked the ball. A copper came up to me and tried to arrest me because he said he'd seen me swearing. "What about the other fifteen thousand in the ground?" I asked. "Don't be cheeky" he said and moved me to the other side of the ground. Another time I saw some Brighton fans beating up a Cambridge fan and the Old Bill pulled up in a police van, saw what was happening and drove off.

Name a player from their team you dislike or hate.   Dougie Freedman. He kept Palace up one season when we were coming up a division. They should have been coming down but his goal kept them up, plus he scored two goals against us once.

Your favourite all time player?   Bobby Zamora. We paid £100,000 for him from Bristol Rovers and he was a goal machine. He scored 31 goals one season and 32 the next. Some people say he hasn't done anything at Spurs and West Ham but I think if they gave him a run out in the team and he scored a few goals, his confidence would come back. If not, I'd love him back at Brighton as he's considered a hero down here.

Have any of their managers, past or present, really got up your nose? Steve Coppell. He got us relegated and then sold Bobby Zamora and then goes off to manage Reading. He's been man-ager of Palace about three times so my conspiracy theory is that he wanted us to go down. Well, he's more a Palace man than a Brighton man isn't he?

The worst song or chant their fans sing?   "You're Just a Team Full of Faggots" or "Does Your Boyfriend Know You're Here?" It gets a bit boring hearing it from every team in our division and some fans think they're being very original by singing it, but sadly they're not.

Your favourite song or chant about them? "P.A.L.A.C.E. Steve Coppell's Got V.D. With a Knick Knack Paddy Whack Give a Dog a Bone, Why Don't Palace Fuck off Home". The other one is "My Old Man said be a Palace Fan, Fuck Off, Bollocks, You're a Cunt".

What's the furthest you've travelled to watch your team? I went to Bolton in the Cup when we took about two thousand up there. We also took about a thousand up to Carlisle, and when the fuel strike was on we took 800 up to Hull City for a Friday night game. We've got a great away support and normally we take away about a third of our home support, which isn't bad for a team that's done relatively nothing for a good few years.

Are you a season ticket holder, and do you think your Club could do more for its fans? Yes I have a season ticket but a lot of the money that comes into the club goes straight back out to help fund our attempt to get our new stadium built at Falmer. The club 'as spent three and a half million pounds just to get it to the planning permission stage. The people who sold the Goldstone ground, and we all know who they were, ripped us off big time. They raped and robbed this club of its heart and soul. If we get this new ground then Dick Knight should be made a saint and have freedom of the city. Excuse the pun but he really is a knight in shining armour! The other robbing bastards were just criminals. The fans here have helped keep this club going and afloat, and we're the most loyal fans in this country.

Have you ever worn a replica shirt? Yes I have.

Have you ever cried at a game? In '92 when we got relegated at Ipswich and twenty thousand Ipswich fans were on the pitch celebrating going up as Champions. I was devastated.

Do you take your children to football? I've got a son who's two and a half and when he's old enough he will be coming with me.

What would you do if a family member married a Rival?
Depends how fit she was. My mum comes from Croydon so we give her stick about being a secret Palace fan, but she denies it.

Do you look out for any other teams' results?   Charlton because a workmate of mine is a Charlton fan, Arsenal because they play such good football and Man. Utd. because I hate them and always check to see if they've been beat.

Are there any other teams you dislike?   Reading because of the Steve Coppell connection. They look at themselves as a big club with a new stadium but they only get gates of around thirteen thousand, hardly the gates of a big club.

If there's one player in the world, past or present, that you could sign, who would it be?   Thierry Henry, a class act.

If you had the choice of the National team winning the World Cup or your side winning the Premiership, which would you choose?   Brighton for the Premiership. To me some of the England players don't seem to have any pride in wearing the England shirt.

Would you ground share with your rivals? No way, every club should have its own identity. We shared with Gillingham for a few years and there was talk of sharing with Pompey a couple of years ago but there'd be trouble every week. It wouldn't work. Let's hope we get the stadium up at Falmer, fingers crossed.